School-wide Systems for Multilingual Learner Success

Innovative and accessible, this book provides a roadmap for designing school environments that address the needs of English learners (ELs). Offering a wealth of resources to support school leaders working with multilingual students, Auslander and Yip explain how a systems thinking approach enables the development of stronger school-wide multi-tiered systems of support and can lead to meaningful, context-specific solutions that set up ELs for success. With vignettes, case studies, and tools for readers in each chapter, the book not only identifies what effective practices look like but also outlines methods to help effectively implement culturally and linguistically responsive teaching. This book covers relevant topics in the field, including

- ◆ Teacher team inquiry, planning, and collaboration
- ◆ Social-emotional learning in planning and instruction
- ◆ Culturally and linguistically responsive, trauma-informed assessment and interventions
- ◆ Effective leadership strategies

Perfect for district, school and teacher leaders, this book includes concrete strategies, tools, and resources for implementing research-informed improvements to support different categories of multilingual learners, including newcomers, students with interrupted education, and long-term ELs.

Lisa Auslander is the principal investigator and senior project director for Bridges to Academic Success, a project of the Graduate Center, CUNY. She is a former teacher, coach, and administrator in New York City schools.

Joanna Yip is a curriculum specialist for multilingual learners and an instructional coach.

Also Available from Routledge
Eye on Education

Engaging the Families of ELs and Immigrants:
Ideas, Resources, and Activities
Renee Rubin, Michelle H. Abrego and John A. Sutterby

Enlivening Instruction with Drama and Improv:
A Guide for Second Language and World Language Teachers
Melisa Cahnmann-Taylor and Kathleen R. McGovern

Leading Your World Language Program:
Strategies for Design and Supervision, Even If You Don't
Speak the Language!
Catherine Ritz

The Classroom Teacher's Guide to Supporting
English Language Learners
Pamela Mesta and Olga Reber

Differentiated Instruction:
A Guide for World Language Teachers, 2nd Edition
Deborah Blaz

The World Language Teacher's Guide to Active Learning:
Strategies and Activities for Increasing Student Engagement,
2nd Edition
Deborah Blaz

An Educator's Guide to Dual Language Instruction:
Increasing Achievement and Global Competence, K-12
Gayle Westerberg and Leslie Davison

Determining Difference from Disability:
What Culturally Responsive Teachers Should Know
Gerry McCain and Megan Farnsworth

Powerful Parent Partnerships:
Rethinking Family Engagement for Student Success
Robert Dillon and Melisa Nixon

School-wide Systems for Multilingual Learner Success

A Roadmap for Leaders

Lisa Auslander and Joanna Yip

Routledge
Taylor & Francis Group

NEW YORK AND LONDON

Cover image: © Getty Images

First published 2022
by Routledge
605 Third Avenue, New York, NY 10158

and by Routledge
4 Park Square, Milton Park, Abingdon, Oxon, OX14 4RN

Routledge is an imprint of the Taylor & Francis Group, an informa business

© 2022 Lisa Auslander and Joanna Yip

The right of Lisa Auslander and Joanna Yip to be identified as authors
of this work has been asserted in accordance with sections 77 and 78 of
the Copyright, Designs and Patents Act 1988.

Library of Congress Cataloging-in-Publication Data
A catalog record for this title has been requested

ISBN: 978-0-367-64193-1 (hbk)
ISBN: 978-0-367-62904-5 (pbk)
ISBN: 978-1-003-12339-2 (ebk)

DOI: 10.4324/9781003123392

Typeset in Palatino
by Apex CoVantage, LLC

Access the Support Material: www.routledge.com/9780367641931

Contents

Tables

Figures

About the Authors

Lisa Auslander, Ph.D., is a former teacher, coach, and administrator who worked in New York City schools and at the district level for over 15 years. She is currently the principal investigator and senior project director at Bridges to Academic Success, a City University of New York (CUNY)–based project at the graduate center, where she leads the work of the curriculum and professional development teams designing resources for teachers of students with limited and interrupted formal education and newcomers. In this role, she works with schools and districts throughout New York State and across the country on their school improvement plans for multilingual learners. She is a licensed administrator and received her PhD in Urban Education at the CUNY Graduate Center with a focus on culturally and linguistically responsive instruction and teacher team practices in the secondary classroom. Lisa also serves as an adjunct assistant professor in educational leadership at Hunter College.

Joanna Yip, Ph.D., has worked in the field of education as a teacher, college counselor, instructional coach, and curriculum specialist with a focus on multilingual learners. She partners with educators to improve curriculum and instruction by integrating language and literacy support for culturally and linguistically diverse students and supports the development of strategic program models for English learners. She has assisted in the implementation of curriculum for newcomers with emerging home language literacy and facilitated professional learning communities for teachers and school leaders. She has experience leading school improvement programs and literacy initiatives in district and charter schools. She has also served as an instructor in teacher education programs.

Foreword

What do multilingual learners need to be successful?
What do educators need to support their multilingual learners?

I have often raised these two questions during preservice and inservice teacher education classes or professional learning sessions to invite reflections from my participants and to embrace the notion that there are no simple answers to these questions. The responses I get are representative of the complex needs and many challenges both multilingual learners and their teachers encounter. The replies are far-reaching yet also surprisingly consistent across the groups of educators I have engaged in this activity. Most teachers are keenly tuned into not only the challenges and perceived obstacles but also the immense opportunities their students are presented with when learning a new language and learning in a new language (Nordmeyer, 2010). They tend to understand – intuitively or consciously – how intricate multilingual learners' academic, linguistic, literacy, and social-emotional development may be and how critical it is for educators to develop a shared understanding of an asset-based pedagogical stance.

Similarly, when teachers' own commitment to strive for success with this student population is explored, they tend to highlight what they can readily offer as well as what types of supports they need from administrators, fellow teachers, parents, and the community, including many tangible and intangibles. These needs range from securing resources and materials that adequately represent their students to time for collaboration, pedagogical knowledge in language and literacy development, additional professional learning opportunities, and personal/ professional qualities such as patience and understanding. There is a need for ongoing and deeper reflections, conversations, and actions about multilingual learners:

There are no easy answers.
There are no quick fixes (even though we often wish for ways to simplify challenging professional situations).
There are no neat toolkits with ready-to-go strategies that work across the board (even though we need actionable recommendations that benefit students in a range of educational contexts).

Often without articulating it, what educators who are committed to equitable learning for multilingual learners need is a dynamic, comprehensive approach to serving the multilingual student populations and their families, one that is built on solid research, evidence-based practices, and contemporary theoretical and pedagogical stances.

On the forthcoming pages of this book, Lisa Auslander and Joanna Yip accomplish just that! For the first time in the professional literature, they present a systems approach to ensure school improvement and organizational coherence in support of multilingual learners. I sincerely celebrate this work as a pathway to bring about lasting change.

This book will help administrators and teachers to collaborate and coordinate their efforts in support of organizational and structural changes that create the conditions for impactful instructional practices. Lisa Auslander and Joanna Yip's powerful, steadfast argument is to focus on four well-supported, collaborative, integrated instructional and leadership practices and use them consistently to bring about much needed, sustained change in multilingual learner education. The carefully coordinated, ongoing practices recommended in this book are designed to support the systemic implementation of culturally, historically, and linguistically responsive and sustaining pedagogies.

Multilingual learners are future leaders who deserve systemic supports rather than limited access to high-quality teachers and teaching and a never-ending cycle of inadequate or ineffective interventions. As David Peter Stroh (2015) suggests, "a few coordinated changes sustained over time will produce large systems change" (p. 15). The four levers for change in this book promise to achieve that: they are meticulously reasoned and supported with powerful stories, research-informed, classroom-based evidence, and carefully constructed tools that facilitate systemic implementation. Wishing everyone reading this book a life-changing experience that will also change our multilingual learners' lives!

By Andrea Honigsfeld

References

Nordmeyer, J. (2010). At the intersection of language and content. In J. Nordmeyer & S. Barduhn (Eds.), *Integrating language and content*. TESOL Classroom Practice Series (pp. 1–13). Teachers of English to Speakers of Other Languages.

Stroh, D. P. (2015). *Systems thinking for social change: A practical guide to solving complex problems, avoiding unintended consequences, and achieving lasting results*. Chelsea Green Publishing.

Acknowledgements

This book is a culmination of conversations with educators, school and district leaders, and teachers we have worked with over the years who have informed our thinking on how to develop schools that are welcoming and thriving communities for multilingual learners. Among them are the educators and experts we interviewed and collaborated with to shape this book who we would like to thank for their valuable contributions: Charlene Nieves, Tim Blackburn, Katya Haggerty, Makini Velázquez, and Molly Ticknor. We acknowledge and appreciate all the educators who preferred to rename anonymous but provided the insights, examples, vignettes, and artifacts here in this book.

Special thanks to Jen Chard, Bridges to Academic Success Research Associate and Director of the Multilingual Literacy Screener at City University of New York (CUNY), who supported the planning, revising, copyediting, and shaping of this manuscript. Additional thanks to other team members Virginia Skrelja and Suzanna McNamara for their wonderful work on language and literacy that informed our thinking and the resource development, particularly in Chapter 4. Thank you to CUNY researchers Elaine Klein and Gita Martohardjono for paving the way for our work in the field with their research about students with limited and interrupted formal education and newcomers.

A special thanks to current and former New York State Department of Education (NYSED) leadership Elisa Alvarez, Angélica Infante-Greene, and Lissette Colón-Collins for prioritizing and expanding the work of multilingual learners both in New York State and other parts of the country through policy work. Thank you to Nancy Cloud, Deborah Short, and Ofelia García for their academic research and professional learning that have raised the importance of culturally and linguistically responsive leadership. We appreciate Andrea Honigsfeld and María Dove's work promoting collaborative team teaching across the country, and

Nell Scharff Panero, who helped lay the groundwork for instructional teams in New York City.

A big thank you to our friends and family who have supported our work and the writing of this manuscript. Thank you to our editor Karen Adler at Routledge for supporting this project.

Most of all we want to acknowledge and dedicate this book to the multilingual learners and families who have contributed to our thinking, who helped us learn how to become more responsive educators, and whose voices are vital in shaping the country.

Support Material

Some of the tools discussed and displayed in this book are also available for download on the Routledge website.

You can access these downloads by visiting www.routledge. com/9780367641931. Then click on the tab that says "Support Material" and select the files. They will begin downloading to your computer.

The resources from the book that are also available online include

♦ Access to an external website created by Lisa Auslander and Joanna Yip, with additional resources for readers.
♦ Downloadable rubrics, tables, and templates for assessment and planning, including:

Table A.1 Self-assessment checklist – Focus on culturally and linguistically diverse students
Table A.2 Self-assessment – Collaboration
Table A.3 Self-assessment checklist – Team leadership and supervision
Table A.4 Self-assessment checklist – Team meeting facilitation
Table A.5 Self-assessment checklist – Planning explicit language instruction
Table A.6 Self-assessment checklist – Designing instructional interventions
Table A.7 Self-assessment checklist – Progress monitoring
Table A.8 Step-by-step protocol for individual student reading observation
Table A.9 Key considerations for using English reading assessments with Els
Table A.10 Vision and purpose

1

Building Dynamic Systems for Multilingual Learner Success

Recent policy history has emphasized the implementation of coherent systems to support students, especially to address key groups such as multilingual learners. However, the educational literature lacks documentation of strategies and descriptions for how to create systems within schools for multilingual learners in the areas of literacy, language development, and social-emotional learning (SEL). Although educators are beginning to understand what is required for multilingual learner success, schools and districts struggle to move from their current reality to one that truly exemplifies the promise of equity in education for all students. In this book, we explore how schools develop dynamic multi-tiered systems that support the academic, social-emotional, and literacy development of English learners (ELs).

While the population of students designated as ELs has grown to 10.1% of public school students in the United States (approximately 5 million students), achievement data show that they lag behind their peers. Nationally, only 68.4% of ELs graduated from high school in the 2017–2018 school year, compared with an 85% graduation rate for all students, according to federal data (NCES, 2020). While there is an overall upward trend in graduation rates for ELs from 57% in 2011 to 68% in 2018 (OELA, 2020), other metrics suggest that ELs are still not getting access to the same opportunities for learning. Only 12% of ELs scored "at or above

DOI: 10.4324/9781003123392-1

proficient" in mathematics in the 8th grade on the 2019 National Assessment of Educational Progress (NAEP, 2019) compared with 25% of students not classified as ELs. The reading results from the NAEP that same year showed only 3% of 12th grade ELs and only 4% of 8th grade ELs scored at or above proficient, despite an already long period when school systems worked toward college and career readiness standards for all students (NAEP, 2019) The percentage of ELs who scored below basic in reading was 72% in the 8th grade and 79% in the 12th grade, an indication that the goals of current reforms in standards-aligned curriculum and accountability for improving outcomes for ELs have not yet been realized (NAEP, 2019).

Since ELs are a growing population of students, it is increasingly important to determine the quality of their learning experience and understand their implications more deeply. Too often, ELs are perceived as a homogenous group without attention to differences in linguistic assets or academic preparation and without an understanding of or value placed on their ability to read, write, and speak in their primary language (García et al., 2008). Furthermore, some ELs are misidentified as students with disabilities or, in contrast, are not referred early enough due to the complexity of assessing their needs (Losen et al., 2015). For students with limited and interrupted formal education (SLIFE), there are not only cultural and linguistic differences, but as with any student, social-emotional factors to consider in assessing the literacy level of older age and adolescent ELs. Newcomers from other countries with interrupted or limited schooling may not have access to transcripts of their schooling experience, so there is often a gap in understanding what their experience of school has been like (Decapua, 2015). Lastly, a significant number of ELs are born in the United States or come from households that are multilingual, including English as a home language (Menken et al., 2012). The needs of such a culturally and linguistically diverse student population cannot be addressed with status quo curriculum and indeed cannot be addressed even through better pedagogical or instructional strategies alone. In addition to these elements, the complexity of serving multilingual learners also requires a systems approach to school improvement.

This book identifies key systems criteria that not only show what effective practices look like but also outline methods used by school and district leaders to manage the challenging processes required for authentic culturally and linguistically responsive teaching to be sustained. We describe our work partnering with schools to build meaningful, context-specific solutions and coherent but dynamic systems to serve ELs grounded in the stories of classroom teachers and school administrators. We are not the first to propose systems thinking as necessary to school improvement, but we make systems thinking come alive through practitioner stories and examples of how system elements interact to create success. The following vignette of a pair of co-teachers at a small elementary school exemplifies the type of stories we share throughout this book, demonstrating how educators seek ways to improve planning and instruction to serve their multilingual students and how systems thinking can help schools improve at a greater scale for a larger number of students.

Students and Teachers in Need: A Vignette

Lois is a general education 5th grade teacher at Garden Elementary who has been teaching for five years but has found that her current group of students consists of an even more diverse student population than in prior years. She has a 5th grade inclusion classroom with 30 students, including five monolingual English students with Individualized Educational Programs (IEPs), ten EL students at varying levels, and 15 English-only students without IEPs. Lois is overwhelmed by the diverse needs of her students. Although she is constantly planning, she often feels like there aren't enough hours in the day to tailor the instruction to meet the needs of all her students. Sometimes she is not sure she even knows how to start.

Lois is happy to have the chance to talk with Maia, the English as a New Language (ENL) teacher, about her ten students who are mostly newcomers, since she has little experience teaching this population and does not really know how to meet their language and learning needs. She also co-teaches three days per week with Joan, a special education teacher, but most of their planning time is once a week during lunch, and that just doesn't seem to cut it. She has no formal planning time with Maia. She shared her frustrations in an interview:

> I didn't get trained in ENL methods, and I'm struggling to know the right ways to support my students. I have many struggling students in the class, and I'm learning how to better differentiate for them. I love working with Maia and getting her input, but it is hard to find a way for her to help since I am doing most of the planning, and she is so busy. The home language assessment I ordered didn't come through for my Spanish-speaking students until late fall, and I couldn't find one in the right language for one of my students. It's hard to know how to see what they know already in order to help them in the right ways.

Maia is a part-time ENL teacher who divides her time between Garden Elementary and a middle school located a mile away. She works 20 hours per week and has a caseload of about 60 students, many of whom are struggling learners, beginner ELs, or newcomers who need a lot of additional support. Many of these students are preparing for state exams and are feeling fear and pressure to do well when they may not be emotionally or academically ready.

A Portrait of Lois and Maia's Students

Maia described two of her students who are both Spanish speakers at different levels. Miguel and Jorge are both the same age and are Spanish-speaking bilingual students from Mexico. Jorge entered the country three years ago, but Miguel just arrived this year.

According to Maia, Miguel is quiet, thoughtful, and interested, and he responds well to one-on-one conversations about content. He has a very strict stepfather who is very dominant in the household. Miguel is quiet and shy about speaking in English. He is not yet speaking in English as a newcomer and is also shy in general, not as talkative as some of his Spanish-speaking peers even in his home language. He is nervous about getting the work right but collaborates with his group, and they are supportive. Maia says:

> When we met, his parents said they felt unsure about his group projects and want him to do a lot more individual preparation for testing so he can succeed. I know it can be challenging to assure them that we are trying to support students in all their needs. Miguel is progressing and writing full sentences. He loves to play sports with a small group of friends on weekends. Teachers notice that he is shy but opens up when he has a friend or two to work with him in class. Miguel is quiet, but he has a lot of resolve. He decided he didn't want to go to a newcomer school with all English learners because he felt he would learn more of the language in having to work with native English speakers. That was his decision.

Maia describes Jorge, on the other hand, as outgoing and social; he switches comfortably between English and Spanish and is fluent and articulate in conversation. When it comes to written language, Jorge both struggles with reading the texts of his 5th grade reading materials in both Spanish and English and often feels disorganized and a sense of frustration with spelling and various forms of written communication. Although he came to the United States in the second grade, he had not been able to receive any Spanish instruction. He did not have a lot of previous schooling in his home country of the Dominican Republic. He received many foundational language supports as he learned English but was also self-conscious about having teachers work too closely with him in the classroom. He was only willing to work with a teacher one on one in an after-school setting.

Maia said, "I have Jorge visit the kindergarten class once a week to be a helper in hopes that he will also learn more from the curriculum and internalize some of the basic phonemic skills he is missing." Jorge also loved to play sports, too. He also very much liked dancing, especially with girls, and had a large group of friends. If he works in a larger group in class, he tends to talk socially for long periods of time so he needs to sit with a group who will help keep him focused. Sometimes he worked alone or one on one with a class partner who is more focused, depending on the task.

Another of Maia and Lois' students, Lila, was a student who was a first-year newcomer. She struggled a bit to adapt to U.S. schooling when she arrived but now at mid-year is having a much better time adjusting to her class. She is a student from Sierra Leone who speaks Krio, a Creole language. She went to school in her home country and is managing well with the transition, even in her first year. Her mother is fluent in English and can help her with the work when she needs help in English, and Lila also has some prior knowledge of English from her mother and from having learned English as a subject in school in Sierra Leone. Lila is very social and has made lots of friends. She is also in the student council and is joining some of the student clubs after school.

Maia concluded, "All three students have different needs. It is amazing how rich their experiences are and how they respond differently to the way instruction happens in class. Their personal experiences become so important to the decisions we make in teaching."

Combatting Teacher Isolation

Lois and Maia do their best to talk in the hallway, after school, or occasionally on the phone or by email about the students. Lois is trying to learn how to adapt her curriculum but is unclear about how to incorporate language objectives into her content objectives for so many different levels of ELs. Miguel, Jorge and Lila each need a different approach to the lessons and subject areas in the class.

Maia has 15 years of experience but feels the constraints of the role she has in the school and the kind of impact she can actually have:

> I work part time and have little time to collaborate with the five to six teachers I work with across the two schools. Often it feels like the kind of work I am doing is crisis

intervention. I feel like I am putting a bandage on a gaping wound. In our elementary school, there is a need to prioritize special education, since we have a 25% special education population. ENL is seen as less of a priority since we have fewer students; however, they have real needs, and I worry about some of them falling through the cracks. I spend a lot of time with the struggling students and newcomers. However, students like Lila could use more support with some of the language skills, and I'm not finding the time since there are more high-needs students in my caseload. I feel that these students are left to sink or swim and that I am drowning.

Lois adds her experience:

The parents are trusting me to do a job – teach their children English but also help them learn and prepare them for the state tests. I'm not sure that I can do that properly without getting the right information about them and the right materials to support their learning. I am overwhelmed and am wondering if I'm in the right job after all. Maia and Joan are great, but I don't have enough time with them for it to really make a difference [in my instruction]. I often feel very alone in this.

Teacher Stories as Public Structures

The struggles of Lois and Maia are not unique. Many teachers express feelings of being overwhelmed by the needs in their classroom and liken teaching to running on a treadmill to keep up with their students' needs but not always having the strategies and resources to support them in the process. In a critical analysis of public education, it is illuminating to see the individual troubles faced by teachers like Lois and Maia as representative of larger institutional challenges and their classroom struggles as symptomatic of the way in which the larger system is functioning and failing (Mills, 2000).

Indeed, the U.S. Department of Education (2010) reports about 13% of the American workforce of 3.4 million public school teachers either moves (227,016) or leaves (230,122) the profession each year. According to the MetLife Survey (Markow & Cooper, 2008), more principals found it challenging to maintain an adequate supply of effective teachers in urban schools (60% vs. 43% in suburban schools and 44% in rural schools) and in schools with two-thirds or more low-income students (58% vs. 37% in schools with one-third or fewer) (p. 6). Even in situations in which there is a co-teaching model in place such as at Garden Elementary, a lack of community or not having a systematic method for collaborating around students' needs may lead to loneliness and dissatisfaction with the profession. In addition, lack of supportive communication and structures may prevent teachers from effectively identifying learning issues that come up in the classroom and impact their ability to set goals with students and build coherent, personalized learning plans. Newer teachers in particular lack experience or knowledge of school-specific resources.

Lois and Maia are not alone in feeling ill-equipped to serve ELs. The Council of Great City Schools found through a survey on serving ELs that only about 51% of educators feel "prepared" or "very prepared" to use specific strategies to ensure that ELs meet the requirements of the Common Core (Council of Great City Schools, 2013). Only 49.1% of public school teachers are certified at the master's degree level to teach ELs. Only 27% of K-12 teachers reported participating in EL-focused professional development compared with 85% of teachers participating in subject-area professional development activities. In the meantime, 73.9% of all U.S. public schools serve ELs in their buildings, and 64.9% of schools offer instruction specifically designed to address the needs of ELs (NCES, 2017). This demonstrates that while schools are enrolling and programming students for services mandated by federal guidelines, teachers are still at a loss for how to address the students' needs in day-to-day instruction.

Lois and Maia are like many educators who need each other's help in making sense of how to assess and inform instruction based on student academic, social-emotional, and cultural needs.

Often teachers have an overwhelming amount of information in the form of state-wide test data, classroom assessment data, or information forged from school inquiry teams or conversations in the hallway. Yet they aren't poised to utilize the information for everyday instruction. At Garden Elementary, there is a great deal of experience and wisdom in the school community in the form of an experienced English for speakers of other languages teacher, a special education teacher partnering with the general education teacher, and a counseling team supporting the students, but there is no system to leverage that expertise to benefit the whole school.

What is lacking in these scenarios is a collaborative team structure that helps the school organization learn, helps educators monitor the progress of students along the way, and shares critical information that increases learning opportunities and support for the students and for the teachers themselves. In addition, many educators are unclear about the kinds of data that could help them make better decisions about academic and social-emotional interventions for the students. How does school leadership begin to put structures in place so such collaboration and coordinated efforts can lead to multilingual learner success? The individual problems that classroom teachers face often need to be solved through school-wide collaboration and organizational systems and structures.

Rather than focus on pedagogical strategies as do many other books in the field on EL education, this book focuses on dynamic systems for school improvement and organizational coherence. It is our belief that even with large investments in professional training, schools cannot leverage teacher expertise without organizational structures. There is now a great deal of empirical research and knowledge that teachers can learn regarding effective instructional principles to serve multilingual learners. Yet this expertise is not translated quickly to classroom activities. The knowledge and evidence for what is high impact is not making their way into classrooms. We believe one important reason this is the case is because schools lack the organizational systems and structures as well as leadership that create the conditions for such knowledge and instructional practices to take hold.

The Necessity of Systems Thinking and the Trap of Looking for Quick Fixes

As educators working with schools to serve their multilingual learners, practitioners often ask us for concrete actions and strategies "that work" in order to replicate them in their own settings. They want quick insights and immediate strategies in response to the increasing linguistic diversity of their schools. The quest for easy fixes and fast results gets in the way of educators engaging in a deeper analysis of the social system within their own school communities. This leads to unsatisfactory outcomes. Instead of replicating ideas presented to them in workshops or recommended to them by other practitioners, educators need a long-term organizational strategy to improve their systems. The quest for isolated strategies leads to schools being continuously unable to build momentum to sustain academic achievement for a broad number of students. They may find idiosyncratic moments of success with one routine or fresh idea, but they cannot achieve results consistently at scale for all of their students. This perpetuates the system's failure to fully educate all multilingual learners.

For these reasons, we rely on a systems improvement framework to help us understand how components of a school are interconnected and the structures needed for large-scale improvement for ELs. A systems-thinking approach lends theoretical framing as well as guidelines for structuring school environments to undergo sustained transformation leading to success for all students (Senge et al., 2012; Gage et al., 2017; Hauerwas et al., 2013). For example, a systems improvement perspective asks leaders to see patterns within their school organization and how various elements and actors are organized within the organizational structure to produce the intended reality for students. There is no doubt in our minds that instructional frameworks and strategies are essential. Many professional learning providers are capable of supporting educators to experience and implement instructional strategies, building broader awareness of the kinds of instructional supports and principles that lead to deeper learning for multilingual learners. We focus this book on highlighting the dynamic systems and structures we have seen help schools to bring that pedagogy to life and sustain high levels of good practice consistently across classrooms within school communities.

Characteristics of Strong Systems in Schools

Systems that produce consistent results have three key characteristics: resilience, self-organization, and interconnectedness or hierarchy (Meadows & Wright, 2008). The internal coherence of the system maintains these characteristics through effective teams, the development of collective efficacy (the ability for an organization as a whole to learn and innovate), and internal mechanisms for accountability (Forman et al., 2017). Using field research and data collection, we gathered examples and stories in the following chapters that draw upon these characteristics to explain what makes particular school-wide systems and structures effective in changing outcomes for ELs.

Resilience is the "measure of a system's ability to survive and persist within a variable environment" (Meadows & Wright, 2008, p. 76) and comes about through interrelated feedback loops that help a system to learn and evolve in response to complexity. When teachers or leaders say that they have had an "influx" of students who are not like those they have served in the past and that they are "struggling" to know what to do, they are referring to a variable environment. Often, these references to culturally and linguistically diverse students are derogatory and deficit-based in nature. The presence of clear feedback loops to monitor the system and signal when a school might need to reorganize its structures in response to new challenges is precisely what is needed when such unfamiliar change is experienced by the actors in the system and leads to organizational resilience. A school system may also choose not to respond, resulting in system failures.

Self-organization is a system's ability to "learn, diversify, complexify and evolve" as a result of clear structures that enable the organization to "make its own structure more complex" (Meadows & Wright, 2008, p. 79). Self-organization allows the elements within the system to come together to solve complex problems and adjust to variability in the environment.

Self-organization within schools means that existing structures, such as strong functioning teams or meeting routines for organizational learning, are able to generate new ways of doing things, experiment and innovate, foster collective efficacy to grapple with challenges, and create new knowledge. This means that even when teachers do not have existing expertise to work with ELs, their existing structures can self-organize to generate solutions. They can do this because when a system is governed by a set of principles and there are structures through which these principles are enacted, systems are able to evolve with the complexity of the world around it (Meadows & Wright, 2008). This self-organization is impossible without effective systems, structures, and teams within an organization. Schools are better positioned to meet the challenge of serving their multilingual learners when self-organization is strong.

Self-organizing systems share a third characteristic: **interconnectedness**. The system is made up of component parts that are highly correlated to produce the behaviors of the overall system. The interaction between system elements within an interconnected web of relations or hierarchy enables the system to function. As such, a system can regulate and maintain itself and enhance the functioning of its elements within a stable, resilient, and efficient set of relationships that produce the intended results (Meadows & Wright, 2008). Interconnectedness is largely a result of the actions and decisions of the school building leader and its leadership team. In order to coordinate the complex system within a school, the leader needs to ensure the stability and the consistency of the school's internal structures. The leader's role is to create interconnectedness between the components of the school system so they can function together as a whole to achieve the goals of the school community. By setting up an interconnected infrastructure, the members of the school community can come together based on their various roles and functions to work toward the common purpose of supporting all students and multilingual learners.

In this book, we provide examples and stories from practitioners of how these characteristics of strong and effective systems manifest in their school communities, what it means for educators to pay attention to these characteristics, and how these characteristics lead to improvements and intended results to better support ELs, particularly newcomers, and other culturally and linguistically diverse students.

What Makes Systems Work for Multilingual Learners: Culturally Informed MTSS

In 2015, the Every Student Succeeds Act, 20 U.S.C. § 6301, (2015), required schools to implement multi-tiered systems and supports (MTSS) as a way to create a model for school services that incorporates academic and social-emotional services through a data-driven but more integrative, holistic approach that includes psychological supports and is designed to meet the needs of all students. The National Association of School Psychologists (2016) defines MTSS as "an evidence-based framework . . . for improving outcomes for all students and for creating safe and supportive learning environments free of bullying, harassment, and discrimination" (p. 1).

As such, MTSS may be a part of education reform and policy, but important is the infrastructure for system resilience, self-organization, and interconnectedness. Integrating culturally-informed MTSS practices provides a more complex lens for considering the whole child, including aspects of race, identity, language, and culture. As a result, a school can develop integrated and dynamic systems that are increasingly responsive to the needs of multilingual learners and their families. Such systems require teachers and schools to use assessments for three purposes:

1. Screening: identifying which students in the general student population might have a problem worthy of further assessment.
2. Diagnostics: identifying what specific instruction students need based on their performance on diagnostic assessments.
3. Progress monitoring: identifying whether the instruction we are providing is working. (National Association of State Directors of Special Education [NASDSE], May 2006, p. 3).

Tiered assessments then inform instruction that also happens in three tiers. The first tier takes place in the general education or inclusion classroom. The second tier takes place either within the classroom in small groups with the support of the teacher or during a small group intervention period. Tier three generally consists of intensive one-on-one intervention (NASDSE, 2006, p. 6).

A multifaceted MTSS approach often suffers in implementation due to a lack of funding or staffing constraints and other factors (Ahram, *RTI Action Network*, n.d.). This is important to identify and to also extend by noting that schools continue to creatively thrive, demonstrating strategies to make MTSS an effective whole-school improvement approach in situations that are anything but ideal. What is promising is that MTSS holds the key components of a system to learn and monitor its overall impact. Tiered assessments and instruction form the basis on which a school organization can understand the impact of teaching and learning, identify the needs of students, and create connections across tiers of instruction within the system to respond to these needs. Truly making MTSS come alive requires an interaction between key actors and elements within a coherent school ecosystem.

For EL instruction, this means that language learning and content instruction go hand in hand through a comprehensive approach (Fisher & Frey, 2010; WIDA, 2013; Richards-Tutor et al., 2016). Tier 1 and Tier 2 instruction most often take place inside the classroom; thus, modeling, inter-visitations, and small group productive work strategies are extremely important to instruction. Discussion is key for ELs and helps scaffold knowledge for all students, especially with increased emphasis on the instructional shifts created as a result of college and career readiness standards that include the use of text-based evidence and argumentative writing. Creating systems and structures to disseminate knowledge and understanding of these practices beyond the language teacher is a critical component for school leaders to consider while building a strategy to support all students.

In our Garden Elementary scenario, successful MTSS would mean that Lois and Maia are scheduled to meet with one another and with a counselor or social worker on a regular basis and talk about each student on a deeper level. In practice, the administration and teachers at Garden Elementary School actually partnered to change their schedule and cultivate facilitative teacher team practices to initiate the use of culturally informed supports in their school the following year. In working with Jorge, it became important for educators to have ongoing communication as issues emerged in the classroom. For example, Lois could tell that Jorge was struggling with her and other students one on one and that he tried to cover up what he didn't understand in both language and content but did not know why these things were happening. The counselor knew more about Jorge's home situation. Communication with the counselor helped Lois and other teachers communicate with Jorge more successfully. They developed a plan with him that Jorge could come to own.

For ELs, this kind of ownership entails having a deep understanding of a student's linguistic strengths and assets in both their primary language and in English and building upon their skills, cultural heritage, and identity. Not only does this suggest a more complex understanding of identity as crucial to the way educators use pedagogy and assessment in the classroom, but it also has significant implications for creating community among educators so they can collaborate and support one another in their understanding of their students, parents, and the community as partners in the instructional and assessment process. As Lois and Maia's experiences reveal, this kind of collaboration cannot be an isolated affair but is planned, intentional, and structured with clear purposes and goals.

On the surface, the organic collaboration among the general education teacher, the English as a second language teacher, and the counselor seems necessary and obvious, yet schools rarely have the structures in place to implement the components necessary for a collaborative and culturally informed teaming process. A school is its own ecosystem, with its own organizing principles, structures, and leadership. When the elements of this system develop resilience, self-organization, and interconnectedness, the school is better positioned to manage the change processes needed to serve culturally and linguistically minoritized students whose needs may be wholly unfamiliar to a given school community. What does the MTSS infrastructure need to prioritize and monitor in order to know if it is adequately serving ELs? How does a school leader define and map out a comprehensive strategy for system improvement to serve multilingual learners? What are the system elements around which a school organization should orient its self-organizing efforts to build resilience? From a systems approach, the starting place for improvement is not merely content expertise or knowledge of the unique needs of ELs but the coordination of teams, collaboration, and system elements.

Four Key Levers for Multilingual Learner Success

Our systems improvement framework is grounded in four major levers to help define these school-wide systems and structure for multilingual learner success. The levers help leaders see what contributes to success for ELs and identify systems and structures to put in place in an evolving educational environment. You'll notice that the levers do not focus on pedagogy and instruction per se but instead show the organizational structures needed for pedagogy and instructional methods to take hold within a community. The four levers help leaders see which elements can be leveraged for improvement and which interconnections can be made stronger to produce the intended results and can help to focus the learning and change needed within the system:

1. *Develop integrated and sustainable team learning* (Chapter 2). These are the collaborative processes and tools schools use to create strong teams, harness the collective expertise of teachers, develop system resilience, and help educators self-organize around instructional principles that lead to innovation and multilingual learner success.
2. *Integrate SEL into school-wide structures for planning and instruction* (Chapter 3). This lever ensures interconnectedness and infrastructure for organizational learning that integrates the instructional and social-emotional needs

of students and collaboration between instructional and counseling staff.

3. *Establish culturally and linguistically responsive data practices to inform teaching and learning* (Chapter 4). This lever is about the practices and systems that serve as feedback loops needed to learn about the strengths and needs of multilingual learners and whether the current system elements are helping students to thrive in school.

4. *Deepen leadership practice and organizational learning for school improvement* (Chapter 5). This lever is required to monitor and coordinate the interconnectedness of all elements in a system so they are aligned to the same purpose and goals for multilingual learners.

Taken together, our systemic improvement framework with these four levers helps leaders visualize and surface where interconnections need to be established or changed to alter the function and purpose of the overall system. We now provide some background information to contextualize the need for and relevance of each of the levers in the context of leading reform for multilingual learner success.

Systems Criteria 1: Develop Integrated and Sustainable Team Learning

In the 21st century, educators are grappling with how to implement culturally and linguistically responsive strategies and a new approach to school collaboration to serve diverse populations (Baecher et al., 2012). This requires a significant shift in commitment, pedagogy, and teacher knowledge to become culturally responsive practitioners (Hammond, 2014). Currently, the system lacks quality instructional resources and assessments for ELs (Gross, 2016). Other than TESOL (teaching English to speakers of other languages) teachers, bilingual teachers, and some literacy practitioners, educators are largely unfamiliar with research-based practices that are effective in scaffolding content and language and accelerating literacy development. Schools need to revamp their instructional guidance system with significant changes to teacher practice if they hope to influence student learning for ELs at the classroom level. Many systems continue to operate under outdated paradigms and perceptions of how to serve multilingual learners and need to shift toward creating environments that support culturally and linguistically diverse students with varied identities and needs to reach academic success (Bianco & Harris, 2014; Richards-Tutor et al., 2013).

As schools organize curriculum and instruction to improve teaching and learning and grow in their ability to respond to the complex needs of multilingual learners, they also need new systems and structures to support changes in practice at the school level. Certainly, large investments in teacher training can help close the gap in teacher knowledge and practice, but educators can also organize learning in new ways through collaboration among teachers to refine their instructional systems using existing resources and assets. Teachers are each other's greatest resources for instructional change. Collaborative structures and intentional use of teachers' work time on instructional teams greatly facilitates a school community's ability to develop innovative teaching practices that benefit not only ELs but all students. The work of instructional teams helps teachers develop collective efficacy to meet the complex needs of ELs and other students they previously thought were unreachable. The kinds of transformations needed in teaching and learning for ELs can take hold when schools take up new processes and tools for collaboration that support educators to grow and harness the creativity of teachers that result in breakthroughs and greater collective efficacy.

Systems Criteria 2: Integrate Social-Emotional Learning Into School-wide Structures for Planning and Instruction

One critical interconnected subsystem within a school is the integration of SEL with other functions within the school community. Maslow's hierarchy of needs reminds us that we must emphasize and create a learning environment that is culturally relevant, important to students, and helps address and nurture more than just students' cognitive needs (Huitt, 2007). Trauma-informed schools are effective at monitoring the needs and supporting students not only in their academic achievement but also in their social-emotional learning needs (Johnson et al., 2019; Morningstar et al., 2018; Orosco & Klingner, 2010). To do this, we need school structures that help surface student needs quickly so that key actors in the system can act upon the information gathered about students' needs and respond with timely, culturally and linguistically responsive, and trauma-informed interventions. The flow of information about students is only as useful as a system's ability to ensure that the information is communicated between critical actors within an interconnected school community and is utilized within clear protocols and guiding principles for SEL.

Systems Criteria 3: Establish Culturally and Linguistically Responsive Data Practices to Inform Teaching and Learning

In the school improvement literature, data practices and using data to "drive" all other parts of the system is the starting place. We present the use of data practices in Chapter 3 after we establish the conditions for teaming and integrated SEL because we have often found that schools need the right collaborative structures in order for data mining to result in high-impact actions and decision-making. When collaborative structures and conditions for effective teaming are in place, school organizations are much better positioned to shift their data practices, review whether they are looking at the right data to begin with for their multilingual learners, and identify the culturally and linguistically responsive data framework that best helps them to determine the impact of their system on student learning.

Assessment practices used for general education systems can often be inappropriate for ELs, particularly newcomer ELs, and as a result, teachers do not have the kind of evidence they need to guide the design of their instruction. School systems are also largely not accustomed to collecting and reporting on achievement in a way that highlights patterns and gaps in equity. Schools are also often not equipped to know what kinds of information to ask about their students to ensure proper program placement of ELs for the necessary services they are entitled to. We have spent the past number of years training practitioners across New York State to use home language diagnostic information for SLIFE identification and program placement, an effort that has required significant resources and funding. Through our work, we have discovered that there is no consistency in the kinds of information that school systems gather about their ELs (Villegas & Pompa, 2020). So much of culturally responsive teaching involves knowing the assets and experiences that ELs bring upon arriving in the United States. Our qualitative research suggests how crucial it is to collect extended educational histories of newcomers to understand what kinds of early interventions are needed when they first enroll in the United States (Yip, 2016) and how much the students' own stories of their experiences as unaccompanied minors can become useful information to inform classroom practices (Auslander, 2019). Yet such information about students is difficult to gather and requires coordinated systems and training for practitioners to know what to ask and look for.

Practitioners also struggle to understand how to make sense of the data they do have available. As a result, they struggle to know where to start even if they are willing to improve their system. Often, the data collected do not provide actionable feedback on the impact of the system on student learning for ELs. Language proficiency and growth is assessed only once a year on state assessments and only allows schools to "autopsy" the impact of implemented interventions after the fact (Kaufman et al., 2012). This means that the system cannot learn quickly about its mistakes or course correct in time to prevent long-term damage. In instances when teachers are gathering formative assessment data, they are often assessing content knowledge or academic skills but do not have a laser focus on assessing language and literacy skills. This is one reason why there is a disproportionate number of students of color and immigrant students who are falsely referred into special education (Losen et al., 2015), thus escalating the need for new ways of pinpointing and prioritizing students' needs (Christo et al., 2014; Russell & Von Esch, 2018; Russell, 2012).

In this book, we focus on how this lever is used within the organizational structures of a school and how leadership practices support the integration of data to inform the day-to-day decisions that practitioners make in order to refine their system for ELs in a more efficient and time sensitive manner.

Systems Criteria 4: Deepen Leadership Practice and Organizational Learning for School Improvement

Discussions of leadership in the field of education often revolve around the characteristics and traits of a leader, but systems thinking requires us to think about the function and role of a leader within the system. A system leader not only uses systems thinking to analyze the behavior and results produced by its school but also determines key strategies to ensure that the elements of the system are functioning and connected in a way that serves the purpose and goal set forth by the school community. As a result, the role of a principal, assistant principal, or district leader engaging in system improvement is monitoring the infrastructure of MTSS and whether the school ecosystem is effectively sustaining its internal resilience, self-learning, and interconnectedness.

Leaders struggle to guide school organizations through complex change processes and often need additional expertise in culturally responsive teaching and language/literacy development, including concrete strategies to integrate into their existing structures. This involves creating structures for organizational learning. Schools only have learning environments where teachers support the needs of multilingual students in a systematic way when those structures are put in place and supported by school leaders (García & Kleifgen, 2010; Hernández Finch, 2012; Moore & Klingner, 2014). A system leader also needs to allocate resources so that crucial elements of a system can be established. For example, leaders who create MTSS implementation plans can help focus closely on the needs of ELs as well as prevent inappropriate referrals (Sanford et al., 2012). These vital system components do not generate automatically in a school ecosystem and should not be taken for granted. They are the result of the vision of school leaders who intentionally create interconnectedness between system elements in order to improve the overall function of the system for ELs.

Enacting MTSS and the Four Levers for System Improvement

Using a systems approach, we describe in each chapter how the levers are integrated within the established MTSS structure, including strategies for coordinating support for ELs within existing school routines instead of leaving that work to do after students are visibly struggling. Each of the following chapters provides vignettes and case studies to engage and guide readers, introduces artifacts from the classroom to reinforce learning, and provides tools for readers to consider in their own planning and practice for school leaders. Through these examples, we hope to show how elements in the system work together and highlight promising practices that leaders may find helpful in planning their own improvement efforts.

Chapter 2, "The Role of Teacher Team Inquiry in Linguistically Responsive Instruction," provides examples of how to set up a teacher team to include a focus on team development, planning tools to support this process, and how to organize around the needs of multilingual learners. Chapter 3, "Integrating Social-Emotional Learning Into School-wide Planning and Instruction," focuses on system-wide collaborative practices that bring together the counselor's perspective and allows for a more holistic approach to student learning by identifying student social-emotional needs as well as concrete strategies for addressing them. Chapter 4, "Building System Resilience with a Multilingual Learner Data Framework," showcases how schools can coordinate the use of literacy, instructional, and social-emotional data sources to develop comprehensive language, literacy, and SEL support for culturally and linguistically diverse students. Chapter 5, "Leading School Improvement for Multilingual Learners," shares leadership stories and practices of four administrators who have made changes in their schools or districts based on a systems thinking approach and what it takes for leaders to lead reform for multilingual learner success.

References

Ahram, R., Stembridge, A., Fergus, E., & Noguera, P. (n.d.). *Framing urban school challenges: The problems to examine when implementing response to intervention*. RTI Action Network. Retrieved March 15, 2015, from http://rtinetwork.org/component/content/article/12/465-framing-urban-school

Auslander, L. (2019). *Creating responsive classroom communities: A cross-case study of schools serving students with interrupted schooling*. Rowman & Littlefield.

Baecher, L., Rorimer, S., & Smith, L. (2012). Video-mediated teacher collaborative inquiry: Focus on English language learners. *The High School Journal*, *95*(3), 49–61.

Bianco, M., & Harris, B. (2014). Strength-based RTI: Developing gifted potential in Spanish-speaking English language learners. *Gifted Child Today*, *37*(3), 169–176.

Christo, C., Crosby, E., & Zozaya, M. (2014). Response to intervention and bilingual learners: Promises and potential problems. In A. B. Clinton (Ed.), *School psychology book series. Assessing bilingual children in context: An integrated approach* (pp. 137–161). American Psychological Association. https://doi.org/10.1037/14320-007

Council of Great City Schools. (2013). *Instructional materials for English language learners in urban public schools, 2012–2013*. https://www.cgcs.org/

Decapua, A. (2015). Promoting achievement for ELLs with limited or interrupted formal education: A culturally responsive approach. *Principal Leadership*, 48–51.

Every Student Succeeds Act (ESSA), 20 U.S.C. § 6301. (2015). www.congress.gov/114/plaws/publ95/PLAW-114publ95.pdf

Fisher, D., & Frey, N. (2010). *Enhancing Roti: How to ensure success with effective classroom intervention and instruction*. ASCD.

Forman, M. L., Stosich, E. L., & Bocala, C. (2017). *The internal coherence framework: Creating the conditions for continuous improvement in schools*. Harvard Education Press.

Gage, N. A., Macula-Gage, A. S., & Crews, E. (2017). Increasing teachers' use of behavior-specific praise using a multitier system for professional development. *Journal of Positive Behavior Interventions*, *19*(4), 239–251.

García, O., & Kleifgen, J. A. (2010). *Educating emergent bilinguals: Policies, programs, and practices for English learners.* Teachers College Press.

García, O., Kleifgen, J. A., & Falchi, L. (2008). *From English language learners to emergent bilinguals: A research initiative of the campaign for educational equity* (Equity Matters, Review #1). Teachers College, Columbia University.

Gross, N. (2016, October 27). *Where are quality instructional materials for English language learners?* Retrieved March 6, 2020, from www.kqed.org/mindshift/46814/where-are-quality-instructional-materials-for-english-language-learners

Hammond, Z. (2014). *Culturally responsive teaching and the brain: Promoting authentic engagement and rigor among culturally and linguistically diverse students.* Corwin.

Hauerwas, L. B., Brown, R., & Scott, A. N. (2013). Specific learning disability and response to intervention: State-level guidance. *Exceptional Children, 80*(1), 101–120.

Hernández Finch, M. E. (2012). Special considerations with response to intervention and instruction for students with diverse backgrounds. *Psychology in the Schools, 49*(3), 285–296.

Huitt, W. (2007). Maslow's hierarchy of needs. *Educational Psychology Interactive, 23*.

Johnson, L. V., Shell, E. M., Tuttle, M., & Groce, L. (2019). School counselor experiences of response to intervention with English learners. *Professional School Counseling, 22*(1). https://doi.org/10.1177/2156759X198594869859486

Kaufman, T. E., Grimm, E. D., & Miller, A. E. (2012). *Collaborative school improvement: Eight practices for district-school partnerships to transform teaching and learning.* Harvard Education Press.

Losen, D., Hudson, C., Keith II, M. A., Morrison, K., & Belay, S. (2015). *Are we closing the school discipline gap?* University of California.

Markow, D., & Cooper, M. (2008). *The MetLife survey of the American teacher: Past, present and future* [A survey of teachers, principals and students]. MetLife, Inc. https://files.eric.ed.gov/fulltext/ED504457.pdf

Meadows, D., & Wright, D. (2008). *Thinking in systems: A primer.* Chelsea Green Publishing.

Menken, K., Kleyn, T., & Chae, N. (2012). Spotlight on "long-term English language learners": Characteristics and prior schooling experiences of an invisible population. *International Multilingual Research Journal*, *6*(2), 121–142.

Mills, C. W. (2000). *The sociological imagination*. Oxford University Press.

Moore, B. A., & Klingner, J. K. (2014). Considering the needs of English language learner populations: An examination of the population validity of reading intervention research. *Journal of Learning Disabilities*, *47*(5), 391–408.

Morningstar, M. E., Lombardi, A., & Test, D. (2018). Including college and career readiness within a multitier systems of support framework. *AERA Open*, *4*(1). https://doi.org/10.1177/2332858418761880

National Assessment of Educational Progress (NAEP). (2019). *National achievement-level results*. www.nationsreportcard.gov/reading/nation/achievement/?grade=8

National Association of School Psychologists. (2016). *Integrated model of academic and behavioral supports* [Position statement]. www.nasponline.org

National Association of State Directors of Special Education and Council of Special Educators (NASDSE). (2006, May). *Response to intervention NASDSE and CASE white paper on RTI* [White Paper]. https://nasdse.org/docs/26_515e0af4-52a4-435f-b1be-505438639cb4.pdf

Office of English Language Acquisition (OELA). (2020). *High school graduation rates for English learners*. https://ncela.ed.gov/files/fast_facts/20200916-ELGraduationRatesFactSheet-508.pdf

Orosco, M. J., & Klingner, J. (2010). One school's implementation of RTI with English language learners: "Referring into RTI". *Journal of Learning Disabilities*, *43*(3), 269–288.

Richards-Tutor, C., Aceves, T., & Reese, L. (2016). *Evidence-based practices for English learners* (Document No. IC-18). University of Florida, Collaboration for Effective Educator, Development, Accountability, and Reform Center. http://ceedar.education.ufl.edu/tools/innovation-configurations/

Richards-Tutor, C., Solara, E. J., Lasted, J. M., Gerber, M. M., Filipina, A., & Aceves, T. C. (2013). Response to intervention for English learners: Examining models for determining response and nonresponse. *Assessment for Effective Intervention*, *38*(3), 172–184.

Russell, F. A. (2012). A culture of collaboration: Meeting the instructional needs of adolescent English language learners. *TESOL Journal*, *3*(3), 445–468.

Russell, F. A., & Von Esch, K. S. (2018). Teacher leadership to support English language learners. *Phi Delta Kappa*, *99*(7), 52–56.

Sanford, A. K., Brown, J. E., & Turner, M. (2012). Enhancing instruction for English learners in response to intervention systems: The PLUSS model. *Multiple Voices for Ethnically Diverse Exceptional Learners*, *13*(1), 56–70.

Senge, P. M., Cambroon-McCabe, N., Lucas, T., Smith, B., & Dutton, J. (2012). *Schools that learn (updated and revised): A fifth discipline field book for educators, parents, and everyone who cares about education*. Crown Business.

U.S. Department of Education, National Center for Education Statistics (NCES). (2010). *The condition of education* (2010–028). Government Printing Office.

U.S. Department of Education, National Center for Education Statistics (NCES). (2017). *Documentation for the 2011–12 schools and staffing survey*. https://nces.ed.gov/pubs2016/2016817_1.pdf

U.S. Department of Education, National Center for Education Statistics (NCES). (2020). *The condition of education 2020 (2020–144). English language learners in public schools*. https://nces.ed.gov/fastfacts/display.asp?id=96

Villegas, L., & Pompa, D. (2020). *The patchy landscape of state English learner policies under ESSA*. Migration Policy Institute.

WIDA. (2013). *Developing a culturally and linguistically responsive approach to response to instruction & intervention (RtI²) for English language learners*. University of Wisconsin: Board of Regents.

Yip, J. (2016). *Educational histories of newcomer immigrant youth: From countries of origin to the United States*. CUNY Academic Works. http://academicworks.cuny.edu/gc_etds/1616

2

The Role of Teacher Team Inquiry in Linguistically Responsive Instruction

In serving English learners (ELs), educators face adaptive challenges for which there are no quick fixes; a change in outcomes requires change in culture, behavior, and organizational structures. Implementing and improving high-quality instruction that truly makes a difference for ELs is the result of painstaking effort on the part of teachers who spend countless hours collaborating with peers, learning new strategies on their own, and tapping into their resourcefulness and creativity that are rooted in a deep desire to serve students. Many educators hope that, with the right support, ELs can thrive in school. Yet not enough teachers are equipped to do the work in a way that is both sustainable and transferable to a large number of students. Even with well-intentioned teachers, systemic racism leads to deficit beliefs and institutional practices that often undermine students' access to a quality education.

For schools to implement and sustain high-quality instruction on a broad scale consistently across classrooms, a team approach is needed for the development of a culturally and linguistically responsive classroom climate and instruction. Individual students may rise above the institutional roadblocks pervasive to poorly coordinated schools, but for entire school communities

DOI: 10.4324/9781003123392-2

to experience significant improvement in student learning, they must work through challenges collectively and systematically. This chapter describes the first crucial high-impact systems criteria for multilingual learner (ML) success: *develop integrated and sustainable team learning*. Here we share the processes and tools that schools use to create strong teams for multilingual learner success. We describe the work of instructional teams and how they support teachers and leaders to enact multi-tiered systems and supports (MTSS) practices that consistently support the achievement and progress of ELs. We describe key actions that make the instructional team a teacher's and school's greatest resource for tackling their toughest classroom challenges.

Why Instructional Teams Matter for Multilingual Learner Success

The instructional team is where data, instructional practices, school culture, and communication about students combine to produce powerful results for students who are served by the team. The instructional team brings together a number of school-wide systems in a coordinated effort to monitor student progress and surface real-time needs in classrooms. Instructional teams meet on a regular basis to problem solve around complex student needs and instructional challenges, which are exacerbated by limited resources. The team gathers to learn new practices, share ideas, analyze curricula, and incorporate social-emotional learning (SEL) into instruction. Teachers learn methods to support language development and high-quality practices through job-embedded professional learning and structured collaboration.

In teams, teachers bring their individual efforts into collaboration with others and build collective efficacy to impact student learning (Bandura, 1993, 1997; Eells, 2011). The team is what enables teachers to support student learning beyond what they could do as individuals. Effective teaming does not just lead to great practices in individual classrooms but also enables a whole school to be resilient in the face of complex challenges (Donohoo et al., 2018). Team learning brings coherence and system-level changes that advance the whole organization. Schools that struggle with student achievement often struggle to put structures in place for teacher collaboration.

The Story of an Instructional Team at Newcomer High

In this chapter, we tell the story of one instructional team at Newcomer High and describe how educators collaborate and engage in instructional problem solving in the everyday life of a school through anecdotes and conversation excerpts collected through observations, interviews, and document analysis. As a team works to improve its MTSS process, academic planning conversations come alive for a group of dedicated teachers serving ELs.

The School and the Instructional Team

Newcomer High is an urban secondary school serving 100% multilingual learners, who have been learning English as a new language for four years or less. At the time of this case study, there were 10 or more languages represented at the small school with approximately 421 students in grades 9 through 12. The student body included 95% ELs, 5% former ELs, and 8% special education students. A total of 57% of the students enrolled were male and 43% were female. The average attendance rate was 85% that year. The student demographics were 20% Asian, 29% Black (primarily Haitian and West African), 38% Latinx, and 13% who identified as White and included students from Yemen. The school had approximately 25 staff members, including the guidance team, a literacy coach, an assistant principal, a principal, a business manager, two special education teachers, and several content area teachers who were dual certified in content and teaching English to speakers of other languages (TESOL). Teacher turnover rate was only 13% in the year prior to this study, extremely low for an urban school.

There were six educators[1] on the instructional team featured in this chapter who regularly attended team meetings. Annie was the science teacher and had worked at the school for eight years. Jeff was a special education teacher, worked across three teams, and had less common planning time than other teachers but showed up as best he could to each meeting. Jocelyn, a seasoned English and English as a new language (ENL) teacher, contributed her experience in teaching English. She worked with the school coach and the English department to integrate writing strategies into the school-wide English curriculum in a more consistent way. Jaime worked at the school for many years, for the first eight years as a social worker and then for the last three years as a social studies teacher. Finally, Gina was a new math teacher hired in the middle of the year. This team reflected many school-wide practices designed to serve their multilingual learners.

Key Actions for Instructional Teams That Make a Difference for Multilingual Learners

When teaming is a planned and intentional element of an organization designed to support growth and resilience, educators engage in learning that is experiential, job embedded, solutions focused, and action oriented. This kind of resilient and sustainable teaming is neither improvised nor coincidental but is the result of actions implemented by school leadership. When leaders intentionally plan and create the conditions for team learning, teams can do more than just tackle instructional challenges. They support practitioners to fully integrate the crucial social-emotional supports that make academic success possible (see details in Chapter 3). The following actions integrate collaboration and sustain learning for teachers to address both the academic and social-emotional needs of ELs:

1. Build the foundation of collaboration.
2. Develop intentional leadership for instructional teams and prioritize team facilitation.
3. Plan explicit language instruction for ELs.
4. Learn from students to design interventions.
5. Progress monitor and determine the impact of instruction.

The benefits of collaboration and the impact of teams on student learning are well documented in empirical research (Eells, 2011).

Teacher collaboration in teams or co-teaching has been identified as a way to develop teacher practice and reinforce learning across disciplines for students (Honigsfeld & Dove, 2016; Murawski & Hughes, 2009; Russell, 2012). In addition to a deeper understanding of language strategies that can be utilized in the content classroom to support multilingual learners, opportunities for teachers to co-plan and collaborate, particularly with English for speakers of other languages teachers or dual licensed teachers, can increase and reinforce language instruction and a deeper understanding of students (Russell, 2012; Honigsfeld & Dove, 2010). Team collaboration has been shown to create coherence in planning instruction for *all* students. In addition to the benefits for teachers, Lave and Wenger (1991) framed embedded team learning as central to students' participation in a group and community as well with their situational learning theory.

Key Action 1: Build the Foundation of Collaboration

At Newcomer High, team collaboration was key to the use of linguistically responsive instructional strategies. Regular collaboration enabled teachers to reflect on classroom practice and reinforce language development for ELs across core subject areas as they enacted selected strategies. Without the team, such efforts would not be sustained nor consistent across classrooms. The presence of psychological safety among the team members was crucial, and the interdisciplinary team functioned as a coherent unit. They laughed together, transitioned to getting serious about the work, trusted one another, and openly shared and received feedback. Intentional and consistent meeting routines (Table 2.1)

Table 2.1 Checklist: Build the foundation of collaboration

• Protect time in meetings for human connection, affection, and joy.
• Establish routines for meetings aligned to the team's purpose and goals.
• Plan an agenda for each meeting aligned to the needs of the team.
• Collectively develop processes for shared decision making to ensure a balance of convergent and divergent thinking.
• Maintain a schedule of recurring team meetings aligned to the team's needs.

created the foundation on which the team maintained its sense of interconnectedness and collective purpose. Jaime, the social studies teacher, talked about collaboration in his school:

> Our school is wonderful about teachers collaborating, in terms of all the materials. For my regular discipline classes of global history, [our team has] a strategy that we try to work through. The way that it's done in each class might change differently because of our personalities . . . but there is very much a focus and strategy that we all have, and we've come together. I can bounce ideas off of them, and they can say, "Well, this worked in my class," but maybe for my students, it might have to be something a little bit different. That helps me with the decisions that I have to make about global history class.

Table 2.2 shows a typical sample meeting agenda from the teams at Newcomer High that reflects some common practices. A meeting protocol for student work analysis can be found in

Table 2.2 Sample team meeting agenda

Meeting Objectives: • To check in about specific student in need • To engage in lesson share so that teacher can receive feedback on design		
Time	**Agenda Items**	**Resources**
5 mins	Review agenda items.	
10 mins	Student "check in" • Discuss current needs of or questions about students with disabilities. • Discuss immediate needs or actions for other students.	Student Individualized Education Program
30 mins	Curriculum share Purpose: Review curriculum and lessons to be implemented with one teacher getting feedback on instructional design. OR Student work analysis Purpose: Determine the impact of a shared instructional strategy by analyzing student work.	Protocol for curriculum share Protocol for student work analysis
5 mins	Review next steps.	

Appendix A. Not surprisingly, instructional teams can transform classroom practice and outcomes for students when they have trusted colleagues who serve as resources for solutions and reliable peers with whom they could bring up questions and challenges (Johnson, 2019). When teachers believe they can bring authentic problems of practice to team members, teams rise together to meet and overcome their everyday challenges. Newcomer High teachers emphasized the value their school community placed on staff and student collaboration. Collective decision making was commonplace and intentional during the course of the workday. Team collaboration contributed to the culture of the school as a whole and was significant in how teachers described their growth and professional learning.

The collaboration among teachers was also present among students. Data from classroom observations indicated that collaboration was a crucial mechanism for students to interact with the teacher and to work with peers to learn new concepts and language. This approach to building a learning community helped the school overcome what Decapua and Marshall (2011) note is an individualistic paradigm of Western schooling. Particularly for newcomers from collectivist cultures, individualistic orientations to achievement can present obstacles to learning in a new school setting. Teachers at Newcomer High intentionally planned collaborative structures to address the cultural needs of students and created ways to show caring. Students talked about the advantages of the supportive culture using terms such as "caring," "helpful teachers," "loving," and "like family."

Key Action 2: Develop Intentional Leadership for Instructional Teams

The strong collaboration on this instructional team was not coincidental. A number of intentional actions and practices were put in place for this coherent team to form. Instead of a rare characteristic found among the most talented of teachers, in schools where team effectiveness is high, collaboration among teachers is in fact the result of a school leader's attention and planning. Teams that transform student learning do so as a result of

Table 2.3 Checklist: Develop intentional leadership for instructional teams

• Create a master schedule that allocates time, space, and staffing for the most optimal teaming structures that align with organizational priorities (e.g., grade-level, interdisciplinary, content, or teams for specific focus areas).
• Provide professional learning opportunities when team leaders, facilitators, or instructional supervisors that lead teams can develop expertise in team development and team coaching.
• Provide ongoing, individualized coaching to team leaders, facilitators, or instructional supervisors to support leadership development.
• Lead each instructional team to establish team-specific purposes and goals aligned to school priorities.
• Name and clarify the role of each member of the team and revise roles as needed.
• Develop a set of shared teaming practices that are used school-wide.
• Monitor the progress of teaming structures throughout the school year and provide interventions as needed when teams face conflict or need to recalibrate.

intentional leadership development, monitoring of team effect-iveness, and common practices shared among the community (Johnson, 2019). On the contrary, teams that fail are the result of a lack of leadership and psychological safety (Edmondson & Lei, 2014). Table 2.3 describes key leadership actions that help establish instructional teams.

The school had a culture of shared decision making, transparency, and communication among staff to voice concerns. The faculty embraced open collaboration because of an established culture of psychological safety and a shared purpose to serve students. The school's leadership dedicated time for instructional teams to meet in the master schedule. Further, students were grouped in cohorts so that instructional teams shared their students. Meeting time was largely dedicated to concerns and agenda items determined by teachers, not by school administrators.

In addition to master schedule design, another factor that impacted team dynamics and the ability for teachers to follow through on decisions was the role of the facilitator. Researchers have written about the role of the team facilitator as crucial to team development. McLaughlin and Talbert (2006) provide different models of design to frame the work of professional learning communities. The process "builds upon teachers' shared professional commitments to serving their students and connects with their interest in particular students in their classroom . . ." (p. 49). This type of group is usually facilitated by a lead teacher or administrator, who serves as a "community coordinator" and whose function is to manage and support the group's learning (Wenger et al., 2003, p. 40). This intentional teaming is especially crucial when practitioners are developing new expertise to support the unique linguistic needs of multilingual learners in complex school settings.

As facilitator, the coach at Newcomer High played a role in supporting the decision-making process of the team, setting the tone and culture. These conditions were created by the principal who worked with the team at the beginning of the year to come to an agreement on the focus of the team's collaboration, as well the coach's role. Many educators struggle in the role of facilitator without training or support. Members of the school participated in two facilitator training programs, one provided by the district and another that the principal had contracted to support the development of inquiry on teams.

With a clear role defined and a shared purpose, the coach used skills in facilitative leadership to anchor team meetings in shared instructional priorities and helped the team decide on concrete actions in classroom instruction for all content areas. In one meeting, although every member agreed to bring in a lesson to share, the facilitator pushed participants to volunteer and commit week by week. This led to cycles of lesson review and then immediate implementation in the classroom so that the teacher would come back to reflect shortly after the implementation of language strategies. You can see the lesson review cycles in Table 2.4.

Table 2.4 Sample three-week sequence of focus areas for team meetings

Week 1	Teacher A presents lesson(s) to the team for feedback/
Week 2	Teacher A executes lesson and team analyzes student work/ Teacher B presents lesson(s) to the team for feedback/
Week 3	Teacher B executes lesson and team analyzes student work/ Team reflects on team progress and decides on the direction of team inquiry/
Cycle continues until all teachers on the team have presented, until students demonstrate they have internalized new skills, or until the team identifies a different learning target through analyzing student work.	

During team meetings at Newcomer High, the coach used an inquiry approach to help advance the instructional discourse and the constructing of knowledge. The team structure helped teachers utilize their knowledge and training to design solutions, address problems in student learning, and determine the effectiveness of classroom interventions. The process required a facilitator to ask the right questions, redirect the conversation as needed, and keep the team on track with the group's purpose and goals. Each meeting was pre-planned with strategic objectives for the agenda, questioning, and tasks for the team aligned to those objectives. The intentional planning and role of facilitator kept the team moving toward and led to strategic actions that would sustain the team's culture of learning and orientation to finding solutions collectively.

Team conversations provide insight into what productive collaboration on instructional teams look like and how these conversations keep the team focused on learning and improving their practice. An important question school leaders need to answer is, *How do we know when instructional discourse on a team has an impact on both teachers and students?* (Caindec, 2017). Often, the team requires explicit teaching of important concepts in instructional design in order to advance the instructional discourse. Teachers at Newcomer High who were more knowledgeable about literacy instruction, like the coach and the ENL/English language arts (ELA) teacher, were able to provide support to other teachers about how to integrate literacy into the content areas, particularly needed for science and math teachers. The data from this team suggest that facilitators help to advance instructional discourse when team facilitators ensure that aspects of collaborative conversations are in place. Table 2.5 describes areas for facilitators to emphasize.

Table 2.5 Checklist: Prioritize team facilitation

• The agenda is well planned and focused on a specific feature of instructional design.
• The tasks and questioning are aligned with the meeting agenda.
• The facilitator closely observes what team members say, think, and do and moves the team to develop a shared understanding, including healthy disagreement.
• The team is focused on evidence of student learning and the current reality.
• The team translates findings into clear actions to advance student learning.

Key Action 3: Plan Explicit Language Instruction for English Learners

With optimal conditions for teaming in place, instructional teams can direct their focus to explicit language and literacy instruction to make an impact on ELs in particular (Table 2.6). According to Lyster (2007), drawing primarily on research from Canadian French immersion classrooms, when teachers do not directly attend to language, students may not have access to the sufficient and extended language instruction necessary to achieve high levels of proficiency. A meta-analysis conducted by Norris and Ortega (2000) showed that older learners of a new language do not achieve high proficiency without direct, explicit instruction, which has been found to be more effective than implicit instruction. The study confirmed the role of explicit instruction as an important factor in teacher planning that later impacted classroom instruction. A linguistic focus can also lead to a stronger culturally responsive stance toward multilingual learners.

High-performing instructional teams select methods and activities, evaluate curriculum and programs, and enable teachers to effectively implement instruction for multilingual learners and remain responsive to their needs. Englert and Tarrant (1995) found that teachers who were given a voice in curriculum development sustained and increased ownership of the design process and implemented changes that were decided by their team, emphasizing the importance of teacher involvement. Although there is less research on teachers of ELs specifically, Peercy et al. (2013), in their study of content area teachers and English as a second language teachers, found that collaborating teachers used tools to articulate and re-conceptualize teaching goals, co-construct

Table 2.6 Checklist: Plan explicit language instruction for ELs

• Establish shared agreement on linguistically responsive planning and explicit language instruction as the focus of the instructional team.
• Determine specific cross-discipline language skills to teach across the curriculum.
• Collectively plan and design explicit language instruction to target language skills.

knowledge, and transform teaching practices to meet the needs of culturally and linguistically diverse students.

The team at Newcomer High saw success in serving new-comer ELs precisely because they placed an emphasis on linguistically responsive planning across the core content curriculum that included explicit language instruction in English throughout the year. Through the team's collaborative inquiry, teachers had autonomy to make instructional decisions, with the facilitator helping the team to devote explicit attention to linguistic form and function as described by Lucas and Villegas in the principles for EL instruction (2010). This focus on explicit language instruction was initiated in response to student needs and motivated by the team's findings from previous cycles of inquiry.

In addition to attention to language development across the year, the team grounded their work in student outcomes within academic disciplines. The team adopted a collaborative inquiry approach that made it possible to identify instructional strategies to address skill gaps in language and literacy (Lesaux et al., 2016; Boudett et al., 2013). The team recognized a significant need to support students with academic writing and chose the Hochman writing program to implement because of its promising results in planning interdisciplinary writing instruction. The methods enabled the team to support the development of specific language structures integrated with content area instruction (Hochman & Macdermott-Duffy, 2015). The team agreed that explicit attention to writing would be a key interdisciplinary strategy of the team.

The team decided that the ELA teacher would model and introduce a strategy to the students first, see how the students reacted to it, and share how she implemented the lesson with the whole team. From there, the other subject areas teachers followed up with activities using the same strategy but using content from their respective disciplines to provide students additional opportunities for practice. Not all of the content teachers felt comfortable introducing the language skills to students, but they felt confident that once the students had exposure in ELA, they could use the same strategies using content from their own discipline to reinforce and provide additional practice both verbally and in writing.

Later in the year, the team decided they could do even more explicit language teaching within the disciplines if they mapped out language skills that the students needed to learn based on their analysis of student work and that they felt were also needed to develop the students' engagement in disciplinary practices. Table 2.7 shows what the team agreed to focus on and integrated within content instruction based on their analysis of student work during the prior semester.

As the team implemented writing strategies and explicit language instruction, the team developed a scope and sequence for language instruction and skills that related directly to each discipline and could also be reinforced across the disciplines throughout the semester. Over time, the team saw how language was a part of every lesson and unit, and the understanding of each student's language development was a routine part of the team conversation. Targeted support and planning for language instruction was effective in both promoting student progress in English and content knowledge simultaneously. Although teachers found they required an even more targeted focus for students with low literacy in home language, a focus on explicit language instruction became a key component of the work that supported student learning across disciplines. Additionally, the

Table 2.7 Sample strategies for explicit language instruction to be integrated with content

Vocabulary	• Use word banks. • Incorporate new vocabulary into sentences. • Create word lists specific to one sentence stem.
Deepen instruction in conjunctions	• More practice with "but" and "so"; less with "because." • Model examples of content sentences for how the conjunction is used. • Use matching activity in which students match the conjunction with the sentence. • Match the subject with the predicate using the appropriate conjunction.
Verb use	• Provide students with content-based model sentences with verbs. Students rewrite the sentence with different verb tenses. • Discuss the function of verbs and teach annotation of verbs in model sentences. • Sort content vocabulary into nouns vs. verbs.

team began to identify the disparate needs of ELs. Newcomer students with emerging literacy skills faced different challenges with English. Students who had mostly grown up in the U.S. but spoke another language at home had yet another set of needs.

Key Action 4: Learn From Students to Design Interventions

Key to a strong teaming structure for multilingual learners is a relentless focus on learning from students, analyzing student work, deconstructing what it tells us about students' strengths and needs, and a habit of staying low on the ladder of inference when doing so. Teams need a shared understanding of students' competence and proficiency in priority language skills and concepts to determine the right course for instruction. Without regularly evaluating evidence of student learning, even high-performing teams can fail to make a real difference for ELs. Table 2.8 provides an overview of key actions to learn about and from students to develop culturally and linguistically responsive practices.

Select Focus Students

Early in the year, the team at Newcomer High established goals in writing skills to guide the team's examination of student work and decided on representative students from different stages on the English language development continuum to track student growth. The team selected Zora,[2] a student with limited and interrupted formal education from West Africa. She spoke several oral languages but was new to reading in print. After being in the school for almost a year and experiencing multiple

Table 2.8 Checklist: Learn from students to design interventions

• Determine a focal group of students to study based on team's priorities and goals.
• Determine and utilize the most effective method to analyze student work that ensures staying low on the ladder of inference and a focus on language practices.
• Make instructional decisions aligned directly with information gleaned from student work.
• Ask the students to articulate their awareness of how and when to use the language skill in order to learn about their comprehension and meta-linguistic awareness.

interventions, she still struggled to access basic literacy skills. There was Dolores, a shy Spanish-speaking student, just emerging in English-speaking skills and who excelled with peer support. Nada, an Arabic speaker, demonstrated growth in English literacy and excelled in science. Fernando, a more advanced student, had strong literacy in Spanish and had demonstrated great gains since the 9th grade. The ENL teacher developed a student profile for each student. (See Chapter 4 for an example of a developed student profile and a tool for creating and using them.) Although the findings from four students were not always generalizable, the team's analysis of student work generated a laser focus on how a particular instructional strategy impacted students at varied levels of learning and helped teachers to consider the design of differentiated approaches. The selection of focus students allowed the team to assess student progress and plan for differentiation. The team members shared knowledge about students and designed entry points to support them that proved beneficial for many other students in the class as well.

Analyze Student Work

In addition to integrating new practices into the classroom, the team's purpose for meeting was largely to evaluate its own impact on student learning. The team allocated substantive meeting time to their most important preoccupation: using student work to deeply understand individual students and determine the differential impact of the strategies they used on students who had varied strengths and needs. The team's discussion of student work incorporated a holistic understanding of students using information such as a student's home language skills, previous academic preparation, personal interests, and academic strengths to contextualize and deepen their analysis. This information was collected by the coach, teachers, and guidance counselors. Teachers raised questions and interrogated their own curricular documents and planning process. Teachers refined lessons based on their reflection, implemented revisions to their methods, and brought results back to the team to discuss. This resulted in an iterative curriculum development process that allowed the educators to more effectively differentiate instruction for a broad range of students.

During one meeting, the team started by looking at student work from a lesson based on changes the team had co-created together for Jaime's history class. The task required students to explain the environmental consequences of oil spills in the Niger Delta. Jaime provided differentiated assessments, and Zora, a student who was new to print, received one that displayed images of mangroves, one before and one after the oil spill. The team analyzed the lesson materials and engaged in a conversation that built their understanding of the students and of linguistically responsive practice as they made sense of the evidence together.

The teachers discussed Zora's work and were able to note her strengths, which included her ability to absorb and discuss content. Jaime observed that Zora was demonstrating small but incremental improvements. They analyzed her use of language in the work sample to consider what language skills she needed more practice with and developed a plan to support Zora in their next steps. Even though the team noticed she did not yet have control of her use of content vocabulary, this did not detract the team from noticing the ideas she was able to communicate.

The facilitator helped the group avoid jumping to conclusions before they fully analyzed what they saw concretely in the student work. The facilitator kept the group focused on evidence in the student work, and the teachers demonstrated their ability to analyze the language practices of the student in very specific ways. The team inferred that the student could advance in both content learning and language skills if she were provided with targeted questions or if she were asked to review her writing and look for content vocabulary. The team developed new ways of thinking to differentiate for students with varying needs and strengths in language development based on a routinized procedure for student work analysis.

Use Student Work To Make Instructional Decisions

To integrate more explicit language instruction in content classes for newcomer ELs and given their focus on writing development, the team needs a methodical approach to integrate writing instruction for all students in a systematic way and then analyze how specific strategies were working for students based on their needs and a specific set of language goals. In Transcript #1, the instructional team reviewed student work from their focus students to evaluate how students grappled with using English conjunctions in complex sentences.

Transcript #1: Instructional Discourse Focused on Language Use

Coach: This is Nada and also Dolores trying to write more complex sentences because it's more open ended. . . . It can become a run on. . . . They are getting it without any prompting, trying to build more complex sentences.

Janine: Yeah, Fernando, too, writing a few run-ons, but he is not year clear how to make a compound sentence. . . .

Coach: Some of the other strategies are about . . .

Jaime: [finishes her sentence] Linkage.

Coach: Some of them are about building clauses; if you think kids are ready for that, then we can design stems related to those.

Angela: We used "since."

Janine: I'm for sticking with "because, but, so" [as my conjunctions].

Coach: Do you all want to try it?

Annie: Yes. [Others nod.]

Coach: Then I would first pick the ones needed in your content area, but then they will need more modeling and scaffolding to know what conjunctions and functions are.

Janine: I found that "while" is hard. . . . We may want to hold off on ones that have multiple meanings.

Annie: "Since" means a time thing, too, but they got it because it was clear it was the same as "because. . . ."

As a result of their analysis, the team realized that at least three students were ready to try complex sentences and were receptive to the use of different conjunctions. The coach encouraged the group to introduce conjunctions that would be most useful for the content being taught in the discipline. This conversation demonstrated how the team used student work analysis to determine the focus of their explicit language instruction and move students incrementally forward toward more complex language skills based on the evidence.

Learn From Student Experiences

To determine the effectiveness of instructional strategies, we can learn directly from students about their experiences by prompting their metalinguistic awareness and determine how students make sense of their own language use. The team of teachers at Newcomer High reviewed student work to better understand how students used language in their science class. They chose a group of four target students who were still developing the skill of using conjunctions in English upon their arrival. Three of the students, Nada, Zora, and Fernando, were shown a food chain concept activity about population in an ecosystem. A teacher interviewed them about their comprehension of the instructions from the past unit and about the uses of the conjunctions they had been taught in class across subject areas. Transcript #2 shows that each student was very capable of using conjunctions and explained why they used them, the key goal of the teachers' explicit language instruction.

Transcript #2: Student Discussion About Language Use

Teacher: What is this [passage] trying to teach us?

Zora: The caterpillar population decreased so that the reason is why . . . *because* . . . this is the reason . . . this is why. . . .

Fernando: The flower population increased *because* the caterpillars decreased. We can plant more flowers or something so there are more flowers. . . .

> The bird population decreased *because* (pause) the caterpillar population helped decrease, *then* the birds population. When the caterpillar population decreases, then the birds have nothing to eat.
>
> Zora: You gotta explain the reason for the decrease in population.
>
> Nada: Sometimes we know something but we don't know why – it helps us use "because" so we know why.
>
> *On the differences between "because, but and so"*
>
> Nada: When you say the negative thing you can use "*but*" . . . like, "I like to read books, but the words are difficult."
>
> Zora: If you want to say "*but*" . . . tomorrow I want to go to school, but my teacher won't come to school. . . .
>
> Teacher: What's the difference between "*but*" and "*so*"?
>
> Nada: What is so . . . if you have a reason and another positive thing to continue . . . so . . . like an example . . ." I like to go to school so I will get enough fun with others."

In this excerpt, Nada best described the differences between the conjunctions, but all four students were able to address the use of "because" and "but" and talked about examples from the curriculum in a detailed way. The students demonstrated adequate understanding of the use of conjunctions as a way to extend and make meaning of the academic content they were learning. Although students' comprehension levels varied, all students spoke to the questions and worked through the exercise, providing some evidence that the team's efforts supported the students' meta-linguistic awareness as they developed English language skills. Student interviews were key to determining whether the instruction had an impact on student learning.

Key Action 5: Progress Monitor and Determine the Impact of Instruction

Throughout the year, teachers tracked the information and progress of students academically, in their SEL, and in their behavioral needs. The teachers made sense of student growth overall and the impact of instruction on student learning over time by tracking the skill development of specific language skills among their selected focus students who represented a continuum of language and literacy. They planned their curriculum around these students as a strategy for expanding differentiation and then evaluated student work for the same students throughout the year to assess how students were progressing. Table 2.9 describes the team's key actions.

Teachers tracked this in a shared document in a database so they could monitor what was happening for each student in different subject areas. The ENL/ELA teacher documented the language growth and interventions used for the students. They used a student information system to track student grades, outcomes, and any issues that came up during or outside of classroom instruction. They shared these data with the guidance counselor who also shared relevant information about students with teachers. When it was time to design Tier 2 and Tier 3 interventions, the document helped determine Tier 1 and Tier 2 interventions, making it clear when Tier 3 or individualized interventions were needed. Because the ENL teacher was present in meetings, data for language growth and development were collected alongside content area knowledge and other skill development. In this way, the team monitored student progress and collected actionable information about ELs than they could get from annual language

Table 2.9 Checklist: Progress monitor and determine the impact of instruction

• Determine the most important data to review on a regular basis and align data systems to elevate these key information.
• Create a system that tracks progress on target language skills over time.
• Use a protocol to help the team unpack trends, connections, and insights from the data to determine impact of their instructional decisions on student learning.

Table 2.10 Student academic snapshot template

Student Name	Academic Strengths	Academic Challenges	Language or Other Modifications or Interventions	Next Steps
ELA/ENL				
Math				
Science				
Social studies				
Elective				

Note: See Chapter 3 for a progress monitoring snapshot for SEL that can be integrated with this tool.

proficiency state exams or even academic achievement data for content mastery.

Table 2.10 shows a shared document in which teachers could insert and share information about students to facilitate collaborative conversations about student progress. This contrasts with the more precise data collection that teachers use to monitor progress in student writing discussed in the next section.

The team used a shared spreadsheet to precisely and intentionally track their analysis of writing skills over time. This tracker helped them see how and if students evolved in specific writing skills the team targeted through explicit instruction and to determine if focus students were learning specific language skills that were prioritized in instruction. Annie described the process the team used to that tracks growth in sentence skills:

> Once at the beginning of the year, maybe in November . . . we looked at student work, and we rated it. There are the different indicators, and then we graded our four target students and those indicators, based on an assignment. So, what we noticed is at the beginning of the year, there were a couple of students who were pretty good at it. They either mastered it or almost mastered it. And then, there were a couple of students who were beginners and students who had not [mastered it]. And then, just recently, maybe a couple of weeks ago, we did it again, with the same students, and we compared it. We're actually looking at student work and rating it.

This approach to analyzing student work called teachers' attention to specific, concrete language practices of students in writing, a departure from the typical use of a general rubric with performance descriptors of categories of skills. This practice led to actionable and impactful instructional discourse among the teachers on the team and was key to the team's development of linguistically responsive practices. Tracking student growth also developed the team's collective efficacy and its own internal resilience in addressing complex instructional problems because they could see the impact of their efforts in a timely manner. The team took time to look at the cumulative impact of their teaching, described in Transcript #2 when the team reviewed and saw a noticeable impact on student learning beyond the target group of students.

Conclusions and Implications for Practice

When effective teams are in place, teams must focus on explicit language teaching in the context of disciplinary learning for the work of the team to meet the needs of ELs. Teams can focus on explicit language teaching with a trained facilitator and with tasks that emphasize language instruction in the disciplines by design. The anecdotes in this chapter show the role of facilitative leadership to support teacher and team development, helping educators stay focused in their collaboration.

Even when instructional teams are well coordinated, they rarely feel deep confidence in their instruction unless they regularly use routines to analyze evidence of student learning. Teams must invest their precious team time in what will have the greatest impact and create a more responsive curriculum and instruction in their classroom. The team structure allows teachers to evaluate student progress, surface student misconceptions, celebrate student successes and progress, and engage in instructional problem solving and collectively improve their curriculum. To reflect and self-assess the development of the instructional teams in your own context, see Appendix A for a team self-assessment tool to build your team's practice of serving multilingual learners.

Ultimately, high-quality language and content-integrated instruction for ELs in an MTSS setting requires thoughtful school-wide shifts in culture, beliefs, and systems. Such substantive change means that teachers and school leaders need to adopt a significant number of new practices and develop new collective efficacy. Schools need teaming structures that empower practitioners to collaborate in order to build such new expertise collectively, not just individually. The work carried out by the team at Newcomer High shows the importance of building team learning to support language development simultaneously with content learning and how the team structure enables teams to accomplish more than individual teachers can by themselves.

Notes

1. All names provided are pseudonyms unless otherwise indicated.
2. All student names are pseudonyms.

References

Bandura, A. (1993). Perceived self-efficacy in cognitive development and functioning. [Abstract]. *Educational Psychologist*, *28*(2), 117–148.

Bandura, A. (1997). *Self-efficacy: The exercise of control*. W H Freeman.

Boudett, K. P., City, E. A., & Murnane, R. J. (Eds.). (2013). *Data wise: A step-by-step guide to using assessment results to improve teaching and learning*. Harvard Education Press.

Caindec, D. D. (2017). *Promoting instructional discourse for secondary teachers of newcomer students: The practice of integrated language and content instruction*. UC Berkeley. ProQuest ID: Caindec_berkeley_0028E_17582. Merritt ID: ark:/13030/m54z0561. https://escholarship.org/uc/item/1vk726v7

Decapua, A., & Marshall, H. (2011). Reaching ELLs at risk: Instruction for students with limited or interrupted formal education. *Preventing School Failure*, *55*(1), 35–41.

Donohoo, J., Hattie, J., & Eells, R. (2018, March). The power of collective efficacy. *Educational Leadership: Journal of the Department of Supervision and Curriculum Development, N.E.A.*, *75*(6), 40–44.

Edmondson, A. C., & Lei, Z. (2014). Psychological safety: The history, renaissance, and future of an interpersonal construct. *Annual Review of Organizational Psychology and Organizational Behavior, 1*(1), 23–43. https://doi.org/10.1146/annurev-orgpsych-031413-091305

Eells, R. J. (2011). *Meta-analysis of the relationship between collective teacher efficacy and student achievement* [Dissertations], 133. https://ecommons.luc.edu/luc_diss/133

Englert, C. S., & Tarrant, K. L. (1995, November). Creating collaborative cultures for educational change. *Remedial and Special Education, 16*(6), 325–336, 353.

Hochman, J., & Macdermott-Duffy, B. (2015, Spring). Effective writing instruction: Time for a revolution. In *Perspectives on language and literacy*. The International Dyslexia Association.

Honigsfeld, A., & Dove, M. (2010). *Collaboration and co-teaching: Strategies for English learners*. Corwin Press.

Honigsfeld, A., & Dove, M. (2015, December/2016, January). Co-teaching: Riding a tandem bike. *Education Leadership, 73*(4), 56–60.

Johnson, S. M. (2019). *Where teachers thrive: Organizing schools for success*. Harvard Education Press.

Lave, J., & Wenger, E. (1991). *Situated learning: Legitimate peripheral participation*. Cambridge University Press.

Lesaux, N. K., Galloway, E. P., & Marietta, S. H. (2016). *Teaching advanced literacy skills: A guide for leaders in linguistically diverse schools*. Guilford Press.

Lucas, T., & Villegas, A. M. (2010). The missing piece in teacher education: The preparation of linguistically responsive teachers. *Yearbook of the National Society for the Study of Education, 109*(2).

Lyster, R. (2007). *Learning and teaching languages through content: A counterbalanced approach*. John Benjamins.

McLaughlin, M. W., & Talbert, J. E. (2006). *Building school-based teacher learning communities: Professional strategies to improve student achievement*. NY Teachers College Press.

Murawski, W. W., & Hughes, C. E. (2009). Response to intervention, collaboration, and coteaching: A logical combination for successful systemic change. *Preventing School Failure, 53*, 267–277.

Norris, J. M., & Ortega, L. (2000). Effectiveness of L2 instruction: A research synthesis and quantitative meta-analysis. *Language Learning, 50*, 417–528.

Peercy, M., Martin-Beltran, M., & Daniel, S. (2013). Learning from each other: Creating a community of practice to support ELL literacy. *Language, Culture, & Curriculum*, *26*(3), 284–299. https://doi.org/10.1080/07908318.2013.849720

Russell, F. A. (2012, September). A culture of collaboration: Meeting the instructional needs of adolescent English language learners. *TESOL Journal*, *3*(3), 445–468.

Wenger, E., McDermott, R., & Snyder, W. M. (2003). *Cultivating communities of practice: A guide to managing knowledge*. Harvard Business School.

3

Integrating Social-Emotional Learning into School-wide Planning and Instruction

To create an environment where multilingual learners can thrive, social-emotional learning (SEL) needs to be an integrative component of schooling for all students, both in and out of the classroom. Instructional practices to support student learning are most impactful within responsive school climates that attend to the unique realities and challenges that culturally and linguistically minoritized students face. Multilingual learners experience great adversity inside and outside of school, so schools must play a central role in providing and coordinating resources for social and emotional support. This begins with recognizing and acknowledging the specific challenges students face to create a frontline of resources and support as students and families navigate school. This applies in particular, but not exclusively, to newcomer families. The COVID-19 pandemic made it apparent how vital SEL skills are to the academic curriculum and are integral to how we teach and facilitate learning and skill building in the classroom.

The project of developing a school culture and climate that is culturally and linguistically responsive and sustaining is the byproduct of intentional school-wide systems and structures and collaboration among professionals who often work in

DOI: 10.4324/9781003123392-3

silos. These schools have structures and practices that not only assist students during crisis but also are trauma informed, sensitive to the impact of systemic racism and low socio-economic status on academic development, and develop students' agency and empowerment. Such schools rely on partnerships among counselors, administrators, paraprofessionals, teachers, and support staff, who form crucial relationship networks that sustain families and students. These schools create and sustain feedback loops in challenging circumstances to support student success (Senge, 1990). This involves knowledge and information sharing in respectful ways among educator teams and incorporating funds of knowledge and family partnerships to serve the child and sustain their learning (Gonzalez et al., 2005).

These school-wide structures for SEL are crucial particularly for students who have adverse childhood experiences (ACEs). In an original study led by the Centers for Disease Control and Prevention (CDC) in 1994–1996, almost two-thirds of study participants reported at least one ACE, and more than one in five reported three or more ACEs (CDC, 2019). In the follow-up study in 2011–2014, almost two-thirds of surveyed adults reported at least one ACE, and more than one in four reported three or more ACEs. These included experiences such as domestic violence, sexual abuse, and so on. The prevalence of negative factors affect multilingual learners in particular, including hate crimes against citizens and immigrants of Asian and Latino descent. Such hate crimes increased by 41% from 2016 to 2019 (Kaleem, 2019), and reported hate crimes against Asians increased 164% in 16 of the nation's largest cities and counties from 2020 to 2021, according to a study from the Center for the Study of Hate and Extremism at California State University – San Bernardino (Levin, 2021).

Counselors and teachers from our partner schools described the challenges that many English learners (ELs) face, particularly students with limited and interrupted schooling, who continue to face barriers after they have emigrated to the United States. These challenges affect their ability to focus and manage the attention needed for learning a new language and participating in school. These challenges include the distinct experiences of refugees or unaccompanied minors who take incredible risks to cross the border and who may be required to show up to multiple court dates or grapple with legal issues related to immigration. Multilingual learners may also experience cultural or linguistic stereotypes that denigrate or impede their learning in addition to socio-economic challenges such as housing transience, as well as the threat of deportation (Auslander, 2019). During the Trump Administration, programs such as Deferred Action for Childhood Arrivals (DACA) were under siege, further endangering undocumented students who had previously been protected. Only in 2020 was DACA finally under consideration to be reinstated (Dickerson & Shear, 2020). Statistics on disproportionality show common patterns. Special education designations for multilingual learners are disproportionate to their numbers; often they are over- or underreferred, and language acquisition is very often confounded with disability (Fergus, 2016; Losen, 2014). Multilingual learners face stereotype threat and discrimination on multiple fronts and can only thrive in environments that care for and recognize their social-emotional needs.

In this chapter, we consider the questions, *How do schools successfully organize with empathy and compassion in response to complex social-emotional needs of multilingual students? How do leaders develop the skills of practitioners and shared practices among school staff with different roles toward a collective, anti-racist vision of coordinated SEL that centers the needs of students and families in the education of multilingual learners?* This chapter outlines key components needed for our second systems criteria: *Integrate SEL into schoolwide structures for planning and instruction,* which includes

◆ Teaming for SEL and academic support.
◆ Effective communication systems to coordinate SEL support.
◆ Equitable procedures for school discipline and referrals.
◆ Trauma-informed professional learning for educators of multilingual learners.
◆ Responsive classroom culture and instructional practices.

These school-wide structures enable schools to integrate SEL in multi-tiered systems and supports in response to student needs, as well as proactively supporting students to develop SEL skills.

With a relentless focus on equity, disproportionality, racial disparities, and other manifestations of institutional racism, schools can use systems for attendance, suspensions, and behavior referrals to understand the student experience in the system. To do this requires an understanding of racially and linguistically diverse student histories and experiences and helping all educators develop the cultural competence to work in complex environments to serve students. Such shifts do not occur overnight and require systematic attention and development through intentional structures.

Teaming for School-wide Academic and Social-Emotional Support

When school staff come together to understand and respond to individual student needs, students experience a climate of support. In Chapter 2, you met a team in an urban school that demonstrated what collaborative practice can look like when focused on instruction. That same group of educators also utilized structures to coordinate non-academic support for students. See the vignette for a snapshot of how instructional teams partner with families and counselors to integrate SEL monitoring.

Integrating a Team Approach to SEL at Newcomer High

At Newcomer High, the instructional team held weekly meetings that alternated between instructional and SEL focus. Guidance meetings were similarly structured with team agendas and routines that enabled them to problem solve around the holistic needs of students. During one meeting, teachers and counselors collaborated with the family to support one struggling student, Juan, who was chronically absent. They brought in the parent to help bolster support for the student and provide a community approach to problem solving for his needs.

Jaime, the social studies teacher, led the meeting since he was able to communicate in Spanish. He began with introductions and then interpreted to Spanish for Juan's mother and from Spanish to English for the teachers throughout the session. He explained that the purpose of the meeting was to talk about Juan's absences and some of his other issues and to discuss a solution. All the teachers spoke during the meeting to contribute their impressions.

The English teacher contributed first in the meeting: "One of the things we're experiencing is that we can't help Juan because he doesn't come to class."

Annie, the science teacher, spoke about science class to the group: "I've taught Juan since last year – what I've seen is a big change." She then turned to Juan. "I remember you were doing a project, and you memorized everything. . . . I noticed that you worked hard to do that presentation to make sure it was good. This year I don't see that same effort from you. In fact, I only saw you three times in the past month."

Gina, the math teacher, spoke next: "I am Juan's math teacher and advisor. He is pleasant and does work some-times. But often he is absent, or when he is here, he is late and leaves class a lot."

Jaime translated for Juan's mother, who went on to say she had been back for only 15 days from the Dominican Republic. She said that one of the main reasons that Juan did not attend school because he felt bad about his lack of education compared with the other students.

She also reminded the teachers that Juan was 17 years old and that she had to be there for her younger children. Often, Juan found it easier to join his father working in con-struction than to go to school. The mother said that she had many conversations with him, that she understood that he was embarrassed, but that he should know that the school wouldn't discriminate against him. After some discussion, the teachers reminded Juan that many of the students in school were older and that they would like to help him if he were willing. Upon being asked about his struggles in school, Juan said, "Sometimes I don't feel like coming all day to school." Caren, the social worker from the school, clarified that one of the contributing factors to Juan's reluc-tance to attend school was the length of the school day.

Their schools close at noon [in the Dominican Republic]. So, Juan, you're not used to it. . . . We need to figure out how to push you to get up and get to school, get you through the whole day. . . . It feels good when you're in school doing the work . . . and you were very proud of it. You can come to my office when you come to school. [Juan nods.] That will be a start. The more you come to school, the more you're going to develop those skills, the more of a chance you're going to be successful. . . . You're going to gain your confidence."

After escorting Juan and his mother out, Caren returned to debrief with the teachers. "Juan has to bring his mom home," she said with a sigh. "That's part of the problem. Will he come back? I hope so. Even if it's 2 p.m., I told him, 'Come back to school just to get a class in.'" By sharing some of the challenges that Juan was having in school during this meeting, Caren served as a mediator to help bridge the understanding among the teachers, the parent, and the student, particularly around Juan's struggle with his transition from the Dominican Republic to the United States.

In addition to facilitating communication across team members, cross-functional teams like this one at Newcomer High regularly bring counseling and pedagogical staff together to problem solve and progress monitor both academic and social-emotional factors. This integrated focus on social-emotional support along with academic achievement helped to ensure that teams did not hold bias about students based on classroom behavior and participation alone. It allowed them to devise interventions for individual students both in and out of the classroom and functioned to streamline communication between staff who held significantly different roles. Even when only communicating virtually via email or through shared documents, teams can monitor, respond to, and coordinate integrated support for students. In schools where ELs are mainstreamed, poorly coordinated schools often fail to share crucial student information about the needs of ELs. A teaming structure enables critical information about students to be shared among teachers and counseling staff so that responses to student needs can be timely, immediate, and culturally responsive.

A Cross-Functional Approach to Tackling Attendance

Attendance is an area where schools see disparities between ELs and other students and requires coordinated systems as well as clear communication channels that are linguistically responsive in order to partner with families and caregivers. Using data from the National Assessment of Educational Progress (NAEP), the Economic Policy Institute found that Hispanic ELs are more likely to miss more days in the school year compared with other subgroups, with a strong correlation found between chronic absenteeism and lower academic performance (García & Weiss, 2018). Such disparities are not inevitable.

To demonstrate how teaming structures can make a difference for ELs, we now describe an example found in another small urban high school, Sunrise Academy, where a cross-functional team came together to tackle chronic absence among their ELs. The school staff were concerned about a 12% decrease in attendance at the start of the COVID-19 pandemic and were struggling to shift these numbers, particularly for their ELs, whose attendance had decreased the most. The counselor leading this initiative to improve attendance cited major leadership challenges, including

1. Teachers who had varied attendance practices and needed a streamlined approach.
2. Students who would remotely check in at inconsistent times for different classes, aggravating the already scattered attendance data.
3. No clear system was outlined for attendance *across* teams despite the hard work of an attendance teacher.

While such challenges were exacerbated and complex to manage during the COVID-19 pandemic, they are also common in schools that struggle to effectively organize systems to address equity gaps in attendance, chronic absence, outreach, and communication with families.

In response, the administrator and counselor leader brought together a cross-functional team consisting of themselves, teachers, attendance personnel, the parent coordinator, the attendance teacher, and parents to find a strategy to tackle this problem. Their analysis of the current state led them to these crucial inquiry questions: How do we influence teachers to become more involved in student and parental outreach when students are not attending their classes? How can we leverage the systems that already exist for tracking attendance (for example, the school database)? How will we do outreach as a team and be more involved in the process? How will we use data to track chronic attendance behavior and create strategies for improvement? As they deconstructed the obstacles in their way, the committee collaborated to develop a process (shown in Table 3.1) to respond to the problem and to track attendance more systematically.

As the team at Sunrise Academy faced the complexity of the situation, they tested the different solutions they brainstormed to see how their actions would have an impact on attendance. During this process, they learned more about their school's system gaps and uncovered additional roadblocks along the way. For example, a few teachers believed it was not their role

Table 3.1 Inquiry process to address attendance challenges at Sunrise Academy

• Use several data capturing systems to begin inquiry into attendance.
• Schedule in-person or virtual home visits whenever possible.
• Analyze the different databases to identify strategies on how to better support teachers to capture attendance consistently.
• Help students mark themselves present by offering a time range to do so (e.g., from 8 to 11 a.m.).
• Use Google Classroom or other assessment data to compare daily attendance with classroom engagement.
• Conduct weekly grade-team meetings to discuss individual students who are absent and are in danger of failing.
• Support teachers in more creative lesson planning, including a variety of styles of teaching to engage students, giving students a sense of ownership and voice that would allow them to be active participants to improve attendance and engagement.

to contact parents of students who were chronically absent. Several individual teachers made consistent errors when taking student attendance. The staff phone log demonstrated outreach, but many parents said they didn't receive those phone calls, so the team needed to establish shared criteria for effective outreach.

As the team learned more about the obstacles their school staff faced, they improved their solutions. To increase efficiency of tracking, the team created a data tracker within their existing database. This allowed them to track attendance for specific students across teams and then allowed multiple people to follow up, instead of just one teacher or staff member. The counselor kept notes about target students that could be viewed by all teachers and staff. Grade-level team members were then able to see the rates of chronic absences and take appropriate action more quickly based on specific information about students. Teachers compiled a list of students who were absent, and the teams cross-referenced those names with Google Classroom to analyze their engagement. These notes were tracked in a common spreadsheet to make the connection between attendance and engagement. One teacher held workshops on modeling creative online strategies for ELs to help address engagement needs.

Through systems analysis and attendance meetings, the cross-functional team was able to support work across school-wide teams by sharing evidence of the gaps in attendance and helping grade-level teams develop personalized solutions to the problem. Teachers who were previously resistant to assisting with attendance outreach began to work more collaboratively with other staff. The leadership of the team supported this work in other ways, too:

1. The right frequency of grade team meetings allowed teachers to collaborate in developing strategies for best practices. An increased number of meetings helped with internal accountability across the school. Leaders set aside overtime pay to both incentivize and compensate teachers for this additional work.

2. The administrator and counselor provided consistent support for the most challenging students to protect teachers from too much administrative work.

3. Having common data trackers allowed the attendance teacher to feel more productive as well as individual teachers on grade teams. This tool built confidence that everyone had the same information about students and that their efforts had a tangible impact on students.

4. In addition to incentives, the leadership team shared acknowledgement and appreciation for the time teachers spent tracking attendance and motivating students to come to class.

As a result of this committee's efforts, attendance increased by 20% over several months, a huge improvement for the school. The school implemented a new way of working that helped maintain accurate data, clear communication among teachers, the guidance team, and administrators and re-established effective practices in outreach to families and students. While these practices were brought about by emergency school closure, it is clear that many schools have learned the importance of teaming and coordination among cross-functional staff members that will likely have lasting benefits on school systems. Both case studies we have presented thus far, at Newcomer High and at Sunrise Academy, demonstrate how school-wide structures enable both instructional and student support staff to communicate, collaborate, and ultimately provide support in integrated ways that advance equity and ensure that multilingual learners can thrive in school. In the next section, we turn to how schools put such school-wide structures in place and what schools can do when the conditions for such structures are not yet in place.

Effective Communication Systems to Coordinate SEL Support

In many schools where school-wide structures for supporting SEL are not already defined, it is necessary for leaders to dedicate time for collective professional learning that establishes protocols and methods for communication and encourages open dialogue between teachers and counselors. This ensures that roles are clear and ways of reporting about student needs are clarified. Schools that struggle to coordinate SEL support for ELs often find that instructional staff, counseling teams, and even administrators are not on the same page about their school's approach to SEL support. Teachers often feel ill-equipped, especially when trauma-informed practices are necessary; counselors may face barriers to communicating effectively with instructional staff; and administrators often fail to communicate with clarity what cross-functional collaboration should look like and work toward in a particular school community. Counselors and social workers hold key insights into what students need and strategies for cultural competency, and teachers hold insights into how students' social-emotional needs and areas of growth impact academic growth. Without integrated systems, these stakeholders who hold crucial information about students cannot merge their expertise to fully support students holistically.

Schools can provide professional learning and school-wide structures that advance an integrated vision of SEL support with both short- and long-term approaches. Even if practitioners are only able to meet once or twice a semester, intentional time for communication and collaboration leads to multilingual learners receiving more appropriate and timely interventions. When teams are clear on how and when to use them, online communication systems can fill the gap for busy school staff with a secure database to store confidential student information. For longer term impact, leaders can organize shared learning experiences that help school staff envision their school community's aspirations for their school environment, provide cultural competency and anti-bias training, and develop shared practices to support SEL.

Table 3.2 shows a model of outcomes resulting from a series of sessions designed to foster strong communication protocols among teams, particularly in handling SEL needs for individual students. As part of a large group professional development series, leaders can bring together cross-functional staff to raise awareness of one another's roles and of the needs of multilingual learners. This sample professional learning example can be adapted for a school community or for a team that includes counselors, social workers, school administrators, paraprofessionals, and anyone else in the school community who wishes to be involved in the SEL needs of students.

Table 3.2 Trauma-informed professional learning series – Sample objectives

Session 1	Session 2	Session 3	Session 4
Objective: Create awareness about each other's roles in the context of SEL (counselor, teacher, administrator).	Objective: Create awareness about trauma in general and specifically how trauma may affect undocumented, refugee, or immigrant students.	Objective: Identify a few key trauma-informed classroom and counseling strategies for supporting students.	Objective: Create a plan of action for collaborative practice.

Sample Professional Learning Activity

Context: In school communities where people are new to working together or haven't collaborated to set protocols, it is important to foster relationships with one another and ensure equity of voice among stakeholders who work with students.

Purpose: Lead an icebreaker to support community building and knowledge and awareness of one another's roles.

Activity: Icebreaker

The icebreaker can begin with introductions of team members using the following questions.

- ◆ What is your name, and what is your role in the school?
- ◆ What made you decide to work in your current role?
- ◆ How do you already collaborate with others in this room?
- ◆ What additional collaboration would be useful?
- ◆ What do you hope to get out of this experience?

Protocols and Norms for Communication and Confidentiality

Once school staff have clarity of their individual roles and responsibilities within their job function, school-wide structures are needed for clear communication channels, protocols for decision making, how to handle critical situations, and norms for confidentiality. With many ELs who face a number of challenges related to poverty, family separation, immigration status, family conflict, depression, or anxiety (Suarez-Orozco et al., 2008), clear protocols and norms ensure that student support is managed with empathy, sensitivity, and cultural competence.

The first step involves establishing norms and expectations for handling critical student issues. School leaders remind staff of responsibilities regarding mandated reporting and confidentiality. Teams need a shared understanding of what is and is not acceptable information to share. Counselors have concerns about the free flow of dialogue and shared experiences that may emerge in classrooms. After experiencing professional learning sessions described earlier, teachers and staff at Woodridge High, a large suburban school with a high percentage of ELs and immigrant students, came up with guidelines to clarify the communication of confidential student information. See sample confidentiality guidelines in Table 3.3.

After deep discussion with staff and among teams, the Woodridge High team developed a communication protocol for how they would log high-level concerns and escalate student issues to improve their internal communication and create a stronghold of support for multilingual learners who may have unique needs and circumstances. If a school already has a strong system of communication, multilingual learners will benefit from the protocols

Table 3.3 Sample confidentiality guidelines

• Respect students' privacy in an educational setting.
• Don't reveal student information in the hallway or in a class, even in a small group.
• Ensure you are in a safe, discreet space before discussing confidential topics with a student.

already developed. The system can be enhanced to serve multilingual learners with the addition of bilingual resources and a culturally responsive approach. This includes using resources that speak to the specific needs of the students in the school, including their race, ethnicity, and home language as well as family and home circumstances, personal interests, and cultural histories.

It is important to note that introducing these kinds of communication processes is not an easy first step, particularly when they have not previously existed. In the case of Woodridge High, there were deep divisions about how to approach sharing student information and how to coordinate with one another. There were many unaccompanied minors who had devastating experiences crossing the border. Some staff and teachers were privy to stories the students had shared. In some cases, the students were even more vulnerable as a result of their experiences, particularly those at risk of deportation. The counselors were very concerned about how their information was discussed and were the catalysts for this set of meetings that would support how team members handled student information and progress monitoring, particularly in the areas of SEL and behavior. The team discussed how to log specific incidents, including signs of depression, attendance issues, harassment, and potential signs of trauma. They identified codes to use to protect student confidentiality and identify risk level. Finally, they set norms around what could be reported in email, the database, on the phone, or in person to help guide the escalation process.

Although this conversation was just a beginning, it raised the team's awareness of policies that protect confidentiality and enabled them to work collaboratively to support student needs quickly. This team worked over several months to redefine and deepen their practices on how to broach issues of trauma with students both inside and outside of the classroom. Scheduling time for this work to take place was often challenging, and the process was delayed at many points. The key to making it work was setting consistent times for the cross-functional teams to meet to set up systems for communication. This can make the difference in a successful process, whether this is 1) progress monitoring

SEL; 2) monitoring attendance, particularly of newcomers who may have special specific circumstances; or 3) behavior referral systems.

Equitable Procedures for School Discipline and Referrals

Integrating SEL into school-wide systems enables schools to be proactive in responding to students' needs and ensures that when school discipline procedures are necessary, the system responds in ways that are culturally responsive and sensitive to the needs of ELs, especially students of color, who are disproportionately subjected to more severe discipline. In another school site further along the continuum in working against issues of disproportionality around race and socio-economic status, a teacher leader, an assistant principal, and the school equity team put together a school referral process to combat some of the recurring challenges faced by multilingual learners. This referral process is reflected in Table 3.4 and can be adapted to your own school site as you consider how you will refer to students who are experiencing behavior challenges that can be affected by multiple factors including social-emotional challenges but may also be misinterpreted through the lens of culture or racial bias. Stage 1 reflects some of the SEL and intervention techniques that the school uses across multiple classrooms to help focus students and develop their ability to communicate, self-regulate, and deal with conflict.

Trauma-Informed Professional Learning for Educators of Multilingual Learners

Ongoing professional learning is needed over time to raise awareness of the specific challenges and adverse experiences multilingual learners face that include trauma, discrimination, depression, and other social-emotional challenges. When schools deepen their shared understanding of issues and needs, they are better equipped to both recognize needs on an ongoing basis

Table 3.4 The school discipline process: A referral system in an urban K-8 school

	Stage 1: Student exhibits problem behavior or need, and teacher submits a referral to the site administrator to consider.	Stage 2: The site administrator receives and evaluates the behavior referral.	Stage 3: The site administrator recommends subsequent intervention services and/or that the student be suspended.
What are your school's policies and practices at each stage?	• The teacher uses a variety of in-class measures (e.g., teacher/student conference, peace corner, reflection sheets, behavioral techniques (expectations outlined in student handbook; mental health referral) to allow the student time to self-correct challenging behavior. • If additional support is needed, all parties involved will complete a written statement describing the incident or challenging behavior. The statement is then given to administration (e.g., principal, assistant principal, dean). • If further assistance is necessary, a student referral form is completed by the teacher or staff member and given to administration.	• Administration receives and reviews the completed referral form. • A conference or discussion is held with all parties involved to address any further details. • Parents are contacted and informed of the situation and possible steps that will be taken. • A mediation is held to try to reach an understanding, resolution, and plan for improvement (e.g., behavior sheet, check-in, student selects a person that they trust in the building to go to when they are struggling with self-correcting their behavior).	• After all measures have been utilized in stages 1 and 2, then administration will collaborate and determine the appropriate action that will be taken for the situation (e.g., guidance, suspension, mental health referral). • Once the administration has made their decision, a parent conference is scheduled to discuss the action that will be taken.
What are some questions about bias belief that should be asked at each stage?	• Do the teacher and student share the same understanding of positive interactions with others?	• Am I collecting an equal amount of information (internal and external factors) that may be affecting the student's behavior?	• Is administration being held to the same expectations of following the ladder of referral?
What are some possible gaps of each stage?	• Teachers are circumventing the ladder of referral. • A posted behavior matrix (school-wide and designated areas) • Sufficient documentation on teachers' efforts in following the ladder of referral	• Review of teachers' documentation of efforts taken to support or manage the student's behavior	• Review of the effectiveness of administrative actions taken • Consistent check-ins with a designated staff member to ensure a successful transition back into the classroom setting

and determine a response. Professional learning sessions can address trauma and how it affects all students and then surface specific needs of multilingual learners. For example, schools can create opportunities for conversation to deepen practitioner awareness of trauma by holding conversations that help them unpack and dispel myths related to the effects of trauma both for adults and children that can get in the way of them responding effectively. Tools such as surveys allow a school community to assess what staff already know and what would be useful to discuss in the future. For more resources, see the list provided in Appendix B regarding where to find information on trauma-informed school approaches.

Leveraging Individual Case Studies

After engaging in a survey of staff to understand what the gaps are in knowledge, we recommend developing professional learning for school staff on trauma-informed education. One way to engage with this topic is to discuss individual case studies to deconstruct the possible effects of trauma and the unique way they affect multilingual learners. Using an anonymized case study fosters conversation about trauma as it manifests itself in concrete terms. The case study of Mateo describes a student from El Salvador who has fled his country as a result of increasing gang violence. His story reflects the growing number of undocumented students and the challenges of unaccompanied minors. If you have a different population, you may want to write your own case study to better reflect the challenges your students face and that you want to highlight in your team discussion. The case study helps practitioners to make connections between abstract understandings of trauma with events and details of an individual student experience that can build empathy, namely, real-life phenomena and behaviors, thoughts, and feelings associated with trauma, so that concrete actions and responses can result. It raises questions to consider in sensitive student cases and adds additional ways of understanding student situations, as well as new ways of thinking about student needs and how to problem solve.

Case Study of Mateo

Mateo is 17 years old and from El Salvador. Mateo is comfortable speaking Spanish and knows a little English after six months in the Bronx, New York. He says that he came with a guide first over the border two years ago from El Salvador after traveling for a week. What made him decide to come is that a police officer at home confused him with a criminal. As a result, he had been arrested and hit on the head, which left a scar. He was released, but there were rumors that he would be sent to prison if they came back for him, despite a lack of evidence. His sister, who lived in the United States, found out what was happening and decided to bring him to the United States illegally. She contacted a guide on his behalf, paid for the journey, and Mateo started the trip. He went through Mexico with fake documents. He passed the border the first time, but when immigration met him, he was caught without a birth certificate. He was sent home but then granted a case to obtain refugee status. After many months, his sister was able to bring Mateo to [the United States]. He lives with her, although his mother is left behind in Mexico. Mateo hopes that he will not only be able to stay but that he will also be able to bring his mother to live with them in the Bronx.

After discussion of this kind of case study, counselors can co-lead a training or team meeting to discuss the way trauma affects learners in general and be sure to use statistics about multilingual learners. One school-based counselor from Woodbridge High describes how one of her students was affected by the challenges of transient housing in her community and also teen pregnancy. Despite the challenges faced by this student, she persevered with the support of the counselor and the school personnel, as well as outside programs.

Reflection of a Suburban High School Counselor

One of my students in particular was a Students with Interrupted or Inconsistent Schooling (SIFE) student. I'll call her Maria. We had sent her to [a vocational school]; she did well, and she had her nurse assistant certificate. . . . But one day she said, "I want to try to graduate from high school," and I said, "Okay, let's come up with a plan." And we sat down and came up with a plan, and it involved summer school and night school. I mean, it was an intense plan, and she already had her baby, but we went with it. She attended summer school and night school. She came back in September, and I realized she was pregnant again. And she was, so now there's a baby number two. I know it wasn't easy for her, but she did it. She graduated last year. And I remember saying, "Oh yeah, that was a big deal." She had no biological parents here; she was living with an aunt, and, from my understanding, that home was just insane, there was a lot of probably illegal activity going on in that home. She did take herself out of it, she ended up finding a boyfriend and living with her boyfriend. She was determined. She went from a beginner to more advanced (on the state test) in less than a year, and she passed her Regents [state content exam]. She was just determined that she was going to do this. And she did.

(Auslander, 2019)

Sharing (anonymized) stories from individuals helps highlight larger national trends that counselors, teachers, and school staff may see often at the school and classroom levels and raises awareness about circumstances faced by many students. In particular, teachers or school staff who have less experience working directly with culturally and linguistically diverse students benefit from understanding the circumstances of multilingual learners. In the case study, teen pregnancy was combined with stereotypes and negative experiences the student faced as a new immigrant to the country, such as language barriers, a lack of family, and a lack of knowledge of the schooling or health system. All of these factors contribute to challenges for students like Maria who need bilingual resources in addition to social integration resources that are available in the larger community surrounding the school.

Responsive Classroom Culture and Instructional Practices for SEL

This last section of this chapter addresses longer term cultural and institutional practices rather than immediate responses to crisis or trauma. In addition to reacting to needs that arise, school-wide structures enable school communities to proactively create resilience and positive behavior that help mitigate the risk factors. School systems can respond to crises and establish foundations for students to thrive, build community, develop solidarity, and feel empowered. Such a sense of agency is present in a school system when practices to support SEL are also embedded in the everyday routines and ways of learning within the classroom.

As with the teacher teams examining literacy in Chapter 2, individuals and teams can teach and monitor SEL skills. In addition to keeping up with areas like attendance and lateness, we can also develop a baseline understanding of what students are experiencing in their families and in their community and what skills they have leveraged to achieve success. School teams can use screeners and assessments such as the Culturally and Linguistically Responsive RTI[2] Planning Form (WIDA Consortium, 2013) to help enable team members to track skills and competencies; there are also individual screeners that many companies have evolved. See Chapter 4 for examples.

Although behavior matters, SEL should not be limited to behavior but rather extended to developing concrete skills that all children and youth need to become successful adults in both personal and professional relationships. For ELs, SEL skills support not only their development but are also necessary to navigate the unique experience of learning a new language, growing up within a minoritized community, or facing cross-cultural challenges as immigrants to a new country. Once we decide what we want to measure, how we monitor progress in SEL is key to helping our students deal with conflict, navigate their school and community, and grow in their ability to respond to pressure in academic, familial, and social relationships.

The Collaborative for Academic, Social, and Emotional Learning (CASEL) framework offers an inventory of SEL skills and curricular resources that are helpful to all students and multilingual learners in five domains: self-management, self-knowledge, relationship skills, responsible decision making, and social awareness (CASEL, 2020). Another key resource for developing life skills includes what is often termed non-cognitive factors (Farrington et al., 2012), or sets of behaviors, skills, attitudes, and strategies that are crucial to academic performance in academic classes but are not measured on cognitive tests. The report broadened the term to go beyond a narrow reference to skills and include strategies, attitudes, and behaviors. All of the tables included in this chapter can help teachers design tools and curricula to support the SEL skills of their students. These social-emotional resources enable multilingual learners in particular to navigate the unique experiences they encounter that are not always visible to or understood by their school communities. In addition, we provide ideas for scaffolds that in particular support ELs who are newer to the country in order to adapt to language needs or their specific challenges.

As with literacy practices in Chapter 2, school leaders can also find ways to work collaboratively with stakeholders around SEL. Teacher teams and counselors can find ways to communicate and support classroom management, improve understanding of student needs, and create more meaningful responsive learning environments as well as interventions. This is not always an easy endeavor. Caseloads of counselors in public schools often exceed manageable numbers in almost every state (Cratty, 2019); however, leveraging collaborative practices, whether remotely through online platforms and tools or through collaborative conversations and team practices, can support timely interventions. See Table 3.5 for an example of a tracking form for social-emotional factors, growth, and challenges for students, extending the inquiry work described

Table 3.5 Individual progress monitoring template for SEL skills

	Teacher or Counselor/ Subject Area	Date and Time Frame	Follow Up
SEL strengths			
SEL challenges or needs			
Modifications and interventions			
Anecdotes			
Teacher and paraprofessional recommendations			

in Chapter 2. Teachers can combine these forms into one spreadsheet to enable teams to track information both on academic skills and also SEL and non-cognitive factors. This can be used as a larger tool integrated with the academic tool or used separately, and it can be integrated into a school-specific database.

In addition to team interaction, the kind of baseline behaviors can be tracked at the classroom level as a way to decide what the focus should be on the SEL strand of the curriculum. This information can also be shared among teams working with the same students.

For example, we recommend creating a checklist of observable behaviors that help assess how students are progressing and if the curriculum addresses their needs to promote 1) collaboration, 2) asking questions, 3) using resources independently from the teacher, 4) respectful interaction with peers and teachers, and 5) managing conflict. Designing your own checklist of specific behaviors will help you assess whether key targeted instructional or SEL skills are being addressed effectively. Table 3.6 provides a sample.

Using a baseline of behaviors and tracking using the SEL domains can help schools, teams, and individual teachers decide what the focus should be for groups of students and individual students in classrooms. In this example, we include use of language as a way to monitor how students are feeling in areas such as risk taking and confidence, which is crucial to the learning process for ELs. The tracking of behaviors in fact also becomes a tool for professional learning because it can be used to surface gaps in practice that teachers and counselors can then use to brainstorm areas for improvement in supporting SEL among their students.

Table 3.6 Sample observable behavior checklist for SEL domains and instructional skills

SEL or Instructional Domain or Subskill	Student Behavior	Observed?/ Notes
Relationship skills: Collaboration	Working together in groups	
Discussion: Asking questions using stems	Asking questions of teacher	
	Asking questions of teaching assistant (TA)	
	Asking questions of peers	
Self-management: Using resources from the physical environment in home language or English	Using anchor charts for support	
	Using dictionary for support	
	Using personal glossary or notes for support	
Relationship skills: Respectful interaction with peers and teacher • Using respectful language • Including others at table in collaboration or discussion • Taking turns talking, sharing • Other behaviors	Respectful interaction with teacher or teaching assistant	
	Respectful interaction with other students	
	On task (group work)	
	On task (independent work)	
Discussion: Using home language (HL) or in English, depending on prompt	Students engaging in conversation on themes from curriculum in home language and/or English.	
Relationship skills: Managing conflict constructively	Students able to work together to resolve problems at the table	

Trauma-Informed Classroom Resources

At the classroom level, SEL and trauma-informed curricular resources can be integrated into academic learning. Using the CASEL domains described earlier, it is possible to integrate activities into literacy or math instruction that target SEL skills as teachers work on instructional strategies with students in the class. Although there are many curricula that can be utilized on a school level, we have included a few activities that can be used for all students, and examples of how to scaffold for multilingual learners are included in Table 3.7.

In presenting these SEL strategies, we acknowledge that supporting multilingual learners with self-management, emotional regulation, a sense of efficacy, and development involves

Table 3.7 Classroom planning tool: Adapting SEL for multilingual learners

CASEL Domain	Subskill: Non-cognitive Factors	Related Strategies for ELs
Self-management	Managing one's emotions	Brain breaks, mindfulness meditation exercises, including translation
	Identifying and using stress-management strategies	Culturally relevant conflict resolution scenarios in home language or English
	Exhibiting self-discipline and self-motivation	Creating checklists in home language and English for projects and posting them; including them in notebooks when developmentally appropriate. Assigning mentorships. Using planning and organizational skills such as creating checklists for organizational routines and protocols, particularly for students less familiar with U.S. schooling.
	Setting personal and collective goals	Setting SEL and academic goals and checking in about them with a peer and/or with the teacher. Conferencing. Including language goals and discussion.
	Showing the courage to take initiative	Using mentorship as a leadership activity or to speak publicly in home language or English. Mentoring a peer in the student's first language as a way to promote bilingualism in the school community.

not just a set of classroom practices but also requires educators and practitioners to listen actively and deeply to the needs that students are communicating. It requires teachers and counselors, who are often white English-speaking women (NCES, 2019), to be deeply reflective of their own biases, the ways in which their practices can trigger fight-or-flight emotional responses from students, and ultimately, check whether their own perceptions may lead to inaccurate understandings of student needs. The strategies we are promoting support students to develop SEL skills, but the responsibility of self-management does not fall solely on the shoulders of the students themselves. The onus is on teachers and counselors to create a safe learning environment that helps students learn these non-cognitive skills and thrive as members of their school community.

The task of self-management is likely more challenging for ELs than many teachers and counselors realize. ELs often experience a lower sense of self-efficacy, a student's confidence in their own ability to achieve their goals, which contributes to lower levels of academic growth (Soland, 2019). Refugee and immigrant students are more likely to experience life-changing experiences and in greater proportions than their peers (Schmidt, 2019). There is evidence that trauma is highly probable during and as a result of the process of immigration itself (Foster, 2001). Hence, the strategies named here are really a starting place to create opportunities for students to increase their participation in the classroom as a result of a psychologically safe environment and relationships with school staff. The roles of the teacher and counselor are to provide these scaffolds and support, gather information about the students social and emotional needs, determine what culturally and linguistically responsive practices may be required, and monitor progress toward social and emotional development. This may require additional attention and support to individual students and adjustments on the part of the teacher.

Using Curriculum to Develop Long-Lasting Social-Emotional Development

Finally, schools can proactively develop systematic ways of explicitly supporting SEL development through the use of self-care curriculum or programs that intentionally teach students concrete strategies that develop social and emotional self-awareness. Rather than addressing CASEL skills as needs arise in particular situations, school-wide systems can integrate systematic teaching of SEL competencies that help students mature over time.

In Kansas City, trauma-informed curriculum and planning has been a district-wide initiative for several years, including transforming schools to provide trauma-informed practices. Schools work in partnership with mental health experts. For example, the district helped integrate a curriculum in partnership with the Truman Medical Center Behavioral Health that allows schools to teach students crisis intervention. Molly Ticknor, prior director of Healthcare Services at Kansas City District and one of the co-developers of a specialized self-care curriculum, shared the goals of these kinds of activities for a school-wide trauma-informed approach. She and her colleague created an informal curriculum to address these needs. In schools in Kansas City where teachers followed this model, they worked together with students to build "Power Plans" to help them identify what causes them stress, what can "help them prepare for a good day," and then to find one thing that can "calm them in the moment." In this activity, students at the elementary and middle school levels drew out their plans with visuals and talked about them with a partner (Lukens & Homiak, 2018). This activity can be adapted for any age from upper elementary to adult and help students identify their stressors and think ahead to plan creative ways to manage their emotions. See Table 3.8 for an example.

As schools implemented these approaches to supporting SEL development, Molly pointed out that students' needs change, so their interventions may change over time; Power Plans are best used as a living, breathing document to be most successful and help students learn what helps them manage their emotions. She also clarified that the idea of the name "Power Plan" came from the students.

Table 3.8 Example student power plan

What causes stress for you? What are your triggers?	Get ready, get set: Things you can do to prepare yourself for a great day.	Calming in the moment: What calms you down in the moment when you feel stressed, angry, or frustrated?
What stresses me out is when I have a lot to do.	Be in a good mood, wake up happy, and be determined to move on.	Listen to some music or go for a walk alone. Be alone for a moment in a place that I feel comfortable.

(Translated from Spanish)

When we were developing the curriculum, we presented this idea to the students and modeled as adults and the teacher modeled. Then, the kids named it. Students all knew their triggers, etc. but often didn't have the vocabulary. Sometimes, we put in visuals if they didn't have the language. One student said after doing the activity. "It's about being in control, right? I have the power." Thus, the term "power plans" stuck and became the way teachers and students referred to the activity.

Molly emphasized that the pre-work for becoming a trauma-sensitive school is to take care of the well-being of teachers. "Teachers need to have their own self-care plan and have a true understanding of what that is in order to implement it with the students." To normalize feelings in school culture, we need to be able to create a shared vocabulary and emphasize working on skills such as regulating emotions, building relationships, and managing conflict as adults so that this emphasis becomes part of the school culture. To develop this culture, there needs to be buy-in from the principal, the superintendent, the team leads, and other school staff; otherwise the change will not happen. Some additional ideas to consider while building classroom culture to integrate SEL are given in Table 3.9.

Table 3.9 Tips for integrating SEL into instruction

• Focus on organizational culture and professional learning that creates a paradigm shift to call attention to student emotions and self-awareness *while* students are learning.

• In the classroom, emphasize teaching moments in reading about history or working on a science project that include an examination of emotions or developing self-awareness. Examples are as follows:
  • Teach about the brain in science class and how the different parts of the brain contribute to our emotions and cognitive activity; integrate project-based learning by building a brain.
  • In social studies, consider reading about a historical leader; have students talk about their emotions and how you think he/she responded in their moment. Molly suggests, "Were they using their wizard brain or their lizard brain?"

• Incorporate brain breaks as part of student learning to help normalize self-regulation routines as part of the day.

Creating a Welcoming Environment for Students and Families

Ultimately, the goal of school-wide systems and structures for SEL is to ensure that when students are learning in classrooms where they spend most of their time in school, they experience a learning environment that manifests the school's best intentions to help students thrive and feel empowered as learners. When broader systems for SEL are in place, the byproduct is classrooms where students feel supported and where teachers feel equipped to use culturally responsive practices that support students to be successful and to feel welcome within the classroom. In such schools, effective SEL classroom practices are not serendipitously found in the classrooms of a few great super star teachers but are the culmination of school-wide systems of structures that bring together teams of school staff with different roles, clear communication procedures, ongoing professional learning, and proactive approaches to SEL development. We end this chapter with examples from two classrooms that detail what classrooms can look like when these strong school-wide SEL systems and structures are in place.

Katya is an ENL teacher of a newcomer SIFE classroom at Newtown High School in Queens, where she has taught for 10 years and served as a dean. Before Newtown, she taught English as a second language in the Ukraine for 10 years. When you walk into Katya's classroom, you will see a welcoming classroom culture built on consistent daily routines that enable students to know what to expect each day and to become accustomed to the activities and flow of each day's lesson. She removes any unpredictability in the sequence and cadence of activities so that she can support students with trauma and enable students in crisis to feel included in the classroom community's cultural practices and norms. In this classroom, students are especially positive about working together collaboratively. One student says, "I feel that other students in the classroom help me to learn more, and we learn together . . . we all work together." Students expressed that they like working in groups with others who spoke their home languages: "When I don't know something, I know there is someone in the room I can ask for help." Overall, being able to work collaboratively helped students work from a place of safety, making it easier to take the risks associated with learning a new language and mitigate feelings of isolation, instability, and overall levels of stress. The use of collaboration in the classroom community helped students to also creatively deal with conflict and confront stereotypes.

Newcomer students who struggle with English can really benefit from using their home language to support English acquisition. Katya provided dictionaries in the home language; labeled common classroom items in both English and home language(s); and, in some cases, incorporated "Walls that Talk" (Bridges to Academic Success, 2018): anchor charts and posters in the physical classroom that guide learning, literacy, and routines in the home language and build student independence in both accessing and using classroom resources (Figure 3.1). Teachers partnered their students with others who speak the same language to increase their collaboration and meaning making. Finally, Katya facilitated the process of students teaching each other about their home language and cultural customs to encourage new learning and respect for one another's culture. We see more about Katya's related instructional practices in Chapter 4.

Engaging Family in Inclusive Classroom Practices

The culturally sustaining practices used by Katya and other teachers in her district extend beyond the classroom. During remote learning, another teacher from a New York City school from District 75 provided highly specialized instructional support for students with significant challenges such as autism spectrum disorders or cognitive delays. In her classroom, Makini created an online tool to help students and their families navigate her classroom, including a classroom library. Each "book" in her virtual classroom is clickable and showcases books under various topics, including "Black Lives Matters," "Libras in Espanol," and inclusive books on autism. She also links to web-based apps that students can use to practice English.

In creating these kinds of resources that engage both students and families, Makini creates opportunities to connect and engage

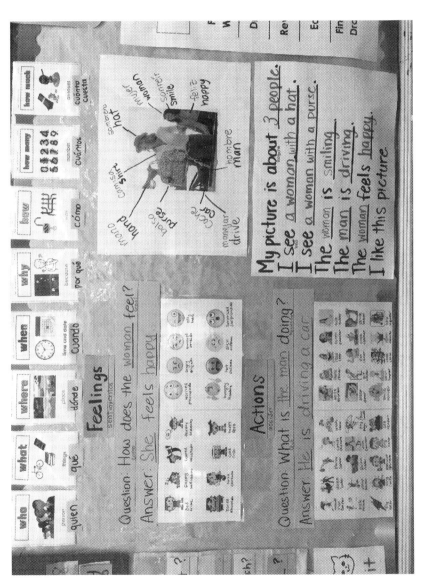

Figure 3.1 Walls that talk image from Katya's classroom

The image shows a photograph of a classroom with supports around the classroom designed for multilingual students, many of whom may be new to the language. These include word walls, visuals, directions in home language, and so on.

families as partners. She and her colleagues began Tech Fridays, particularly during the pandemic, when remote learning became the norm. These sessions helped orient parents to the various technologies used in her school, including Google Classroom. Their team conducted a significant amount of outreach to recruit parents, including weekly calls and check-ins and invitations. She designed the sessions so that parents would provide input on what was taught in the workshops for the next time, which increased engagement and attendance. The partner teachers also included a web page with other resources including information on home language and translation support. Other schools included a significant amount of outreach to families not only to provide educational information but also to provide and coordinate food to families in need who were affected by unemployment and lack of income. Like Katya, we introduce more of Makini's instructional approaches in Chapter 4.

Conclusions and Implications for Practice

In both Katya and Makini's classrooms, we see examples of the welcoming and collaborative environment that supports individual students to manage the effects of trauma or disability, in collaboration with counselors and families. This is the painstaking result of multiple school-wide systems and structures coming together to produce such a learning environment that both responds and develops SEL in children and young people. As educators who have interacted with many different kinds of schools, we have often found the school environment and climate to be critical to a community's efforts to support culturally and linguistically diverse students. These school environments often seem to exist due to the sheer efforts of good-hearted and dedicated educators who work in those buildings, but when we look closely, we see that those committed educators are actually systematically collaborating, communicating, problem solving, and learning together continuously over time to build toward a vision of their school community that is humanizing, compassionate, and anti-racist. Their intentional planning, strategizing, and building of school-wide structures result in such transformational communities that make a difference for multilingual learners. This SEL system is the foundation on which all instructional initiatives must be grounded in order to see results in academic achievement.

Another lesson learned here is that creating incentives, building in time to develop strong relationships and buy-in from staff, can make all the difference in building and sustaining teams. As we move into Chapter 4, we consider how to integrate SEL and family engagement in ways that are integral to instruction and plan it as part of the tiered intervention plan. We can also consider how to tackle larger leadership challenges by creating systems that will better address and target the needs of the students, through interdisciplinary teamwork. Taking an inquiry, data-driven approach is key whether we are working on academic, attendance, or SEL issues.

References

Auslander, L. (2019). *Creating responsive classroom communities: A cross-case study of schools serving students with interrupted schooling.* Rowman & Littlefield.

Bridges to Academic Success. (2018). *Walls that talk* [Video]. https://bridges-sifeproject.com/walls-that-talk/

Centers for Disease Control and Prevention (CDC). (2019). *Preventing adverse childhood experiences: Leveraging the best available evidence.* National Center for Injury Prevention and Control, Centers for Disease Control and Prevention. www.cdc.gov/violenceprevention/pdf/preventingACES.pdf

Collaborative for Academic, Social, and Emotional Learning (CASEL). (2020). *SEL: What are the core competence areas and where are they promoted?* https://casel.org/sel-framework/

Cratty, D. (2019). School counselors matter. *The Education Trust.* www.schoolcounselor.org/getmedia/b079d17d-6265-4166-a120-3b1f56077649/School-Counselors-Matter.pdf

Dickerson, C., & Shear, K. (2020, December 4). Judge orders government to fully reinstate DACA Program. *New York Times.*

Farrington, C. A., Roderick, M., Allensworth, E., Nagaoka, J., Keyes, T. S., Johnson, D. W., & Beechum, N. O. (2012). *Teaching adolescents to become learners: The role of noncognitive factors in shaping school performance* [Critical literature review]. University of Chicago Consortium on Chicago School Research.

Fergus, E. (2016). *Solving disproportionality and achieving equity: A leader's guide to using data to change hearts and minds.* Corwin Press.

Foster, R. P. (2001). When immigration is trauma: Guidelines for the individual and family clinician. *American Journal of Orthopsychiatry, 71*(2), 153–170. https://doi.org/10.1037/0002-9432.71.2.153

García, E., & Weiss, E. (2018, September 25). *Student absenteeism: Who misses school and how missing school matters for performance* [Report]. Economic Policy Institute. epi.org/152438

Gonzalez, N., Moll, L., & Amanti, C. (2005). Preface. In N. Gonzalez, L. Moll & C. Amanti (Eds.), *Funds of knowledge: Theorizing practices in households, communities and classrooms.* Routledge.

Kaleem, J. (2019, November 12). Latinos and transgender people see big increases in hate crimes, FBI reports. *Los Angeles Times.* www.latimes.com/world-nation/story/2019-11-12/hate-crimes-fbi-2018

Levin, B. (2021). *Report to the nation: Anti-Asian prejudice & hate crime.* Center for the Study of Hate and Extremism, California State University. www.csusb.edu/sites/default/files/Report%20to%20the%20Nation%20-%20Anti-Asian%20Hate%202020%20Final%20Draft%20-%20As%20of%20Apr%2030%202021%206%20PM%20corrected.pdf

Losen, D. J. (Ed.). (2014). *Closing the school discipline gap: Equitable remedies for excessive exclusion.* Teachers College Press.

Lukens, L., & Homiak, C. (2018, March). Incorporating trauma-sensitive practices in K – 12 classrooms with refugees [Presented paper]. *The annual meeting of TESOL*, Chicago, IL.

Schmidt, L. M. (2019). Trauma in English learners: Examining the influence of previous trauma and PTSD on English learners and within the classroom. *TESOL Journal, 10*(1), e00412. https://doi.org/10.1002/tesj.412

Senge, P. M. (1990). *The fifth discipline: The art & practice of the learning organization.* Currency Doubleday.

Soland, J. (2019). *English language learners, self-efficacy, and the achievement gap: Understanding the relationship between academic and social-emotional growth* [Research brief]. The Collaborative for Student Growth at NWEA. www.nwea.org/content/uploads/2020/03/researchbrief-collaborative-for-student-growth-english-language-learners-self-efficacy-and-the-achievement-gap-2019.pdf

Suarez-Orozco, C., Suarez-Orozco, M., & Todorova, I. (2008). *Learning a new land: Immigrant students in American society*. Belknap Press of Harvard University Press.

U.S. Department of Education, National Center for Education Statistics (NCES). (2019). *Number and percentage distribution of teachers in public and private elementary and secondary schools, by selected teacher characteristics: Selected years, 1987–88 through 2017–18* (Table 209.10). https://nces.ed.gov/programs/digest/d19/tables/dt19_209.10.asp

WIDA Consortium. (2013). *Culturally and linguistically responsive RtI planning form*. https://morethanenglish.edublogs.org/files/2013/09/RtI2-Planning-Form-for-ELLs-WIDA-1y4ki5q.pdf

4

Building System Resilience With a Multilingual Learner Data Framework

As schools recognize the gap in opportunities for English learners (ELs), a multi-tiered systems and supports (MTSS) approach that relies on relevant data shared among educators provides crucial information needed to develop culturally responsive practices and system resilience. The third criteria in our system improvement framework is *establish culturally and linguistically responsive data practices to inform teaching and learning*. The goal of this criteria is to learn about students' strengths and needs and improve the system by exposing inequity. In this chapter, we present a multilingual learner data framework that brings together language and literacy assessment data with cross-cultural and social-emotional learning (SEL) data to inform the design of instruction and learning environments for ELs to thrive in school. We present classroom examples of explicit teaching strategies for ELs and how instructional practices combine with SEL and culturally responsive practices to support newcomers with confidence to learn language, content, and literacy skills. This integration of literacy and SEL information is also crucial to help long-term ELs to regain faith in a system in which they have experienced a history of repeated failure and discouragement.

DOI: 10.4324/9781003123392-4

The Data We Really Need for Equity and Multilingual Learners

Schools need data systems that integrate accurate and relevant information for students who are multilingual to gain clarity about how their system is responding to the various needs of ELs. Schools often need to shift data practices from those that historically only served a general education population to using precise information regarding ELs (see Table 4.1 for details).

An equitable data system that serves ELs places students at the center so that their needs are prioritized *at the start*, *at each level*, and *at every phase* of data analysis (Hawn et al., 2020). Integrating various data about students and determining which assessments provide relevant information to practitioners is one way this systems criteria fosters equity.

Although they are widely used, English proficiency assessments or reading screeners do not take a student's entire linguistic repertoire into account. From students who use multiple languages that are primarily oral to students who are highly literate in multiple languages, multilingual learners bring a rich set of

Table 4.1 Shifts toward culturally and linguistically responsive data practices

Shift from:	Shift to:
Shift from using only standardized assessment data to . . .	• using localized assessments and tools that directly surface the immediate needs of ELs; or • consistently disaggregating achievement data by EL subgroups.
Shift from collecting and analyzing data periodically to . . .	• frequently interpreting formative assessment data. • routinizing responses and key actions to be taken after data analysis.
Shift from having a few select specialists review data specific to ELs to . . .	• implementing school-wide organizational structures that facilitate the use of data within instructional teams.
Shift from using assessments and tools that are utilized for all students to . . .	• appraising assessments and tools for cultural and linguistic accuracy.

language and literacy practices drawn from their cultures and traditions. Consequently, some experts in the field critique the use of standardized assessments for their lack of linguistic responsiveness (Abedi, 2006). This leaves practitioners with insufficient tools and a reliance on human interpretation. Given the kind of implicit bias that exists among educators (Benson & Fiarman, 2020) and lower academic expectations teachers have of students classified as ELs (Umansky & Dumon, 2019), we support the use of a tiered assessment framework that integrates varied sources of information for a more holistic picture of student needs and to guide the decisions of educators.

Culturally and Linguistically Responsive Data Practices: A Multilingual Learner Data Framework

Assessment systems typically tell us more about the effectiveness of a school organization than about the students themselves. A tiered assessment system solves for some of the limitations of standardized assessments and centers multilingual learners because the goal is to gather information about needs and assets of the student. The Multilingual Learner Data Framework in Table 4.2 provides an overview of key information to form a profile of a student's language, literacy, educational, and social history.

Taken together, the data in this framework support instructional and programmatic decisions for teaching and learning within a school's curricular system, and ultimately, determine the efficacy of the system in responding to student needs. We now turn to examples of how schools have used multiple forms of data to learn about students, their families, and their communities.

Intake, Enrollment, and Placement

When there is a coordinated intake and enrollment system, schools can quickly allocate resources and design targeted interventions for students in an equitable manner and share key information about ELs to relevant stakeholders upon their first day of school. During intake and enrollment, one key question is

Table 4.2 Multilingual learner data framework

Data Source	What It Can Be Used for	Examples of Assessments
Home language	• Placement in intervention programs • Developing instructional scaffolds in core classes • Flexible groupings in inclusion classrooms or Tier 2 interventions	• Multilingual Literacy Screener (Martohardjono, 2015) • Star Reading Spanish (Renaissance, 2015) • ENIL, Foundational Skills Toolkit (Sanchez et al., 2013) • Woodcock-Muñoz (Woodcock et al., 2017)
EL assessment data	• Use for EL identification • Use for EL annual progress monitoring • Determining proportions of EL subgroups (i.e., newcomer, developing, long-term EL, students with limited and interrupted formal education, dual identified, reclassified) in the population • Determining language assessment data over time, including rates of reclassification or exiting EL status and so on	• WIDA screeners (WIDA, n.d.) • New York state identification test for English language (NYSITELL) and New York state English as a second language achievement test (NYSESLAT), (New York State Department of Education)
English literacy assessment	• Monitoring reading behaviors and abilities in English	• General running records • Independent Reading Leveled Assessment (IRLA) (Hileman & Cline, 2014) • F&P (Fountas & Pinnell, 1996) • MAP Growth (Northwest Evaluation Association (NWEA), (2000)
Student work analysis	• Identifying what students can and cannot do related to targeted writing skills.	• 6+1 CUNY Rubric (based on Coe et al., 2011) • Hochman writing assessments (Hochman & Wexler, 2017)
Educational and social history	• Information about family background, student interests, language, characteristics, and work and leadership skills.	• Interview protocol • Oral questionnaires

(Continued)

Table 4.2 (Continued)

Data Source	What It Can Be Used for	Examples of Assessments
SEL assessments	• Assessing student SEL skills helps schools decide what SEL skills to focus on. • Self-reported data such as surveys for older students, performance measures, or teacher reporting measures	• SEL Assessment Guide (CASEL, 2019) • Devereux Student Strengths Assessment (LeBuffe et al., 2009) • Devereux Early Childhood Assessment (LeBuffe & Naglieri, 1998) • SEARS: Social Emotional Assets and Resilience Scales™ (Merrell, n.d.) (See Durlak et al.'s (2015) *Handbook of Social and Emotional Learning* for more information.)
Comprehensive tools for academic and SEL factors	Gathering information about learning modalities: • learning environment • academic achievement and instruction • oral language and literacy • personal and family • physical and psychological data • previous schooling • cultural factors	• WIDA Tool, adapted from Hamayan et al. (2013)
Attendance	Student attendance in a school database on a daily basis, in specific classes. This can be used to: • Identify obstacles to attendance. • Create follow up plans to consult with parents, family, and guardians. • Work in interdisciplinary teams to monitor data from individual students and across grade teams.	• Local attendance database

What do we know about a student's strengths in their home language(s) and student's educational history? Whether there is a standardized home language literacy screener like the Multilingual Literacy SIFE Screener used in New York State (Martohardjono, 2015), or a locally designed assessment, the goal is to learn about a student's linguistic assets in all of the languages in their linguistic repertoire.

Because teachers are understandably preoccupied with classroom setup at the beginning of the year, clear procedures and practices for intake and EL identification make the administration of each state's mandated assessment more effective to identify students who are bureaucratically determined to be ELs. The quality of the intake process is dependent on each school's context and how administrative teams organize, coordinate, and facilitate assessment and enrollment processes. EL practitioners can provide specific recommendations for individual cases that require troubleshooting or communication with caregivers. In addition to assessing home language literacy, it can be beneficial to use observations and SEL screeners during the intake process as well to build knowledge about a student's strengths and needs in SEL skills. This can also better equip teachers and staff to make intervention plans and designs both in and out of the Tier 1 classroom.

The Role of Intake and Data for Programming at Learning Academy

An example of a streamlined intake and enrollment system for ELs is a Bridges to Academic Success (n.d.) partner school, Learning Academy, which has a dedicated enrollment team. A small school with fewer than 500 students and 100% s ELs, Learning has a smooth-running system developed over many years of enrolling recently arrived students coming from multiple countries of origin and speaking more than 13 languages. For the majority of students, Learning Academy is their first school in the United States. In 2018, 38 students transitioned from a local middle school, but 73 students were new arrivals, making up 66% of the total incoming student body. The school created an exhaustive enrollment process that included home language literacy assessment.

Each year, approximately 20% of newly enrolled students were on or close to grade level in their home language; about 80% of students were below 3rd grade literacy in their home language based on the state home language screener. More than 90% of the first 100 students who dropped out of school had low literacy as a contributing factor. As a result, the leadership team revamped the enrollment process to provide support for this student population from the start. They implemented an academic risk questionnaire administered to all incoming students, a literacy and numeracy assessment, and a dedicated enrollment team to document and monitor student needs. The principal described the system:

> One of the most important things that our enrollment team does for all students is administer an academic risk questionnaire. Through this questionnaire, the social support system begins to assemble for that individual student. Our enrollment team consists of our counseling staff and our key support staff in the main office, who are establishing relationships with our students and their families from the very beginning, all coordinated by our licensed ESL [English as a second language] coordinator and testing coordinator.

In addition to administering multiple types of screeners, the school individualizes the intake process by gathering a dossier of student information related to academic strengths and needs as well as social-emotional skills and autobiographical history. The principal continued:

> We are getting information about whether or not the student has missed any instruction: How many days a year? How big were their class sizes? Were there any interruptions due to teacher strikes or political strife? We ask a variety of questions, including if there were medical issues that prevented the student from going to school. All these factors help us develop a profile of what will be needed for the student. [The team will] acclimate the family and acclimate the student to a new academic schedule, figuring out whether or not the student belongs in the regular classes or in the year-long Bridges [Sheltered] SIFE program.

Using these different screeners early in the year helped the school's enrollment committee make decisions about placement into specific courses, communicate critical information about students to teachers, and develop strategies to serve students at the start of their high school career. This was particularly beneficial for students who need targeted literacy support in their first year of high school as a dropout prevention strategy.

One of the teachers described the importance of the enrollment process for high-risk students with interrupted schooling, who often need five years to graduate from high school. Students and caregivers may be reluctant to enroll in a sheltered program with instructional interventions for their first year out of fear of falling behind. They needed to better understand the power of interventions to provide academic foundations that would set them up for success for the duration of their high school career. A teacher from the enrollment team described her experience:

> I do literacy testing and the initial testing. I have also done the initial counseling with them. In the classroom, I make sure that I'm transparent about a lot of things: their level, [that] they all share common goals, they all share common setbacks. So, I think creating a community is super important but also letting them know the purpose of what they're doing and why they're here.

Over time, Learning Academy created a successful intake process that 1) utilized state and local screeners, 2) established clear procedures for administering the screeners, and 3) was implemented by a dedicated team that clarified expectations and transparency about the school's program options for parents and caregivers.

Developing Learner Profiles

After the intake and EL identification process, schools can ask, *What can we learn about our student's needs from historical, demographic, and standardized assessment data?* (Linquanti, 2001; Hopkins et al., 2013). Performance on state language proficiency assessments (not just in one year but over time), the initial time of EL identification, and the number of years the student has been classified as an EL all provide a picture of the pace at

Developing responsive classroom communities for SLIFE & Newcomer learners

Bridges to Academic Success: Building a student profile

Instructions: Please fill out the following template to create a profile of the SLIFE learner in your classroom. You can do this in team meetings with other educators who may know the student and pass it on to future teachers who will work with the student. This may develop as a working document.

The principles behind this profile document stem from the *Six Principles of Exemplary Teaching of Language Learning* (Short, Becker, & Hellman, 2018), particularly principle 1, know your learners, and principle 6, engage and collaborate within a community of practice. In addition, we draw from Zacarian (2013) around the following ideas about learning:

1) Learning is a sociocultural process: we can understand a student from their personal, social, cultural and world experiences;
2) Learning is a developmental process: we consider a student's age, prior knowledge, language proficiency and exposure to literacy practices;
3) Learning is an academic process: we consider grade-level academic content and linguistic knowledge required in school to succeed;
4) Learning is a cognitive process: we develop teaching and learning strategies with the intent of developing and building higher-level thinking skills.

Through building profiles for our students collaboratively with others, we can help prevent misidentification around special education referrals and plan more holistic and appropriate instruction and intervention plans.

Details	Description
Demographic info.	
Name/pseudonym	
Gender/pronouns	
Age	
Home country (and city if known)	
Background/story: How did the student come to the US?	
Home language	
School language in home country if the student went to school	
Academic skills: Content & language	
Home language literacy level for all tests taken (reading comprehension, math)	
Reading foundational skills or comprehension test in English within first 3 months (F&P, IRLA, etc.)	
Observations on writing in home language or writing screener *Attach a writing sample in home language or English, and a sample of work in math	
Observations about English oral production upon arrival	
Observations about home language oral production	
Notes about English proficiency, including pragmatics, fluency, accuracy	
Any skills that were developed outside of a school context that can be transferred to academic skills	
Social-emotional	
Personal/social interests (personal interests, hobbies, strengths, dislikes)	
Behavioral/social skills	
Any other info you want to include?	

Figure 4.1 Developing a student profile

which the system has effectively (or not) empowered a student to develop academic literacy skills in English and whether past programming was effective. Such historical information should be interpreted in the context of a student's educational history from country of origin to the present. Students may need explicit language instruction if there are indications that literacy development has stagnated, such as designation of long-term EL status, the same proficiency level on a state exam for more than 2 years in a row, or gaps in schooling contributing to low literacy in home language.

By creating time and space for classroom teachers to make sense of, easily access, and utilize these data during curriculum design, lesson planning, and decision-making processes, schools can expand the differentiated supports they provide. We recommend schools create a student profile about individual students that include a student's educational history, learner characteristics, literacy data, and more. See the sample student profile worksheet in Figure 4.1.

Language and Literacy Data: Classroom Progress Monitoring Strategies for Multilingual Learners

As we build learner profiles to understand the complex needs of individual students, the next crucial questions are: *What can we understand about a ML's strengths and skills in reading, writing, speaking and listening? How do we know if a student is able to comprehend a text in English?* While language proficiency assessments have a reading component, they only assess reading in English and may not include assessment of component skills needed to read fluently in English. Educators of ELs need a data source that enables them to quickly identify component skills that ELs might be struggling with when learning to read in English because access to reading comprehension is foundational to academic participation. General reading screeners that provide overall measures of reading comprehension are not particularly accurate in determining the reading comprehension of newcomer ELs. However, English reading diagnostics that provide insight into particular English syllable types, oral fluency, comprehension, vocabulary, and if needed, the student's ability to match sound to symbol and phonemic awareness provide actionable information for designing instruction, determining specific skills to teach with content instruction, and if specific areas require systematic intervention and explicit instruction.

Throughout multiple years of implementation, we have trained teachers to use reading observation protocols which consist of one-on-one assessments of a student's oral reading fluency in English reading comprehension. Such assessments gather critical information and capture a powerful assessment of the student's linguistic strengths and reading practices, including how they use home language when reading. It can help teachers build a strong relationship with the student, which is especially critical for ELs to persevere and maintain stamina when learning to read and write in a new language. A reading observational protocol helps teachers to determine which skills students are ready to learn next, design targeted reading instruction in the context of disciplinary learning and thinking, and implement multi-tiered interventions. We believe this approach to be a promising practice that supports students to develop academic literacy skills and ensures that instruction is linguistically responsive to students' assessed strengths and needs. See Appendix C for a sample protocol and key factors to consider when administering reading assessments to ELs.

Recording conferences with students and then analyzing the recordings with other teachers allows for more accurate interpretation of reading and writing assessment data. For example, one may record students completing a reading or engaged in collaborative text-based conversation. Teachers can see the correlation between what students can do on reading comprehension tasks and what they can do with language in different modalities. Verbal responses during collaborative discussions or a conference with teachers provides key information about students' comprehension and their grasp of new language skills. They also allow teachers to see what students can express orally and whether they can express the same in written form. Teachers can use such information to identify specific literacy routines that target what students are ready to learn next and create opportunities for practice over a period of time.

The main barrier to this practice is the time needed for implementation, but the return on investment is relevant and actionable information for teachers. Schools can use a reading observation protocol with a small group of focal students to develop teacher expertise initially before they create a broader strategy for implementation. See Figure 4.2 for a teacher engaging in a sample reading conference with a student.

Sample reading conference

Student: *16 years old, female, newcomer and SLIFE, from El Salvador. Arrived in the United States 6 months ago. Multilingual Literacy SIFE Screener Spanish, Level 2 (2nd grade and below)*

Text level: *Y in the Independent Reading Level Assessment; Level C in Fountas & Pinnell*

Key skills *to assess: active reading strategies and initial consonants*

Context: *Based on an initial inventory of the student's vocabulary and reading strengths in English, the teacher chooses a text level for the conference. Using the Independent Reading Level Assessment, the teacher asks the student to choose a short text from a few options, all of which are at the same reading level. After spending a few minutes sharing some laughs and jokes with the student about how she competes with her brother, who is another student in the class, the teacher begins the reading conference.*

Teacher: I have two texts for you. Text A and B. Choose one that you like and you will read it in your head first. Then, you will read it to me. Which one do you like?

Student: (smiling and pointing) This one.

Teacher: (The teacher points to the text and title.) The title is, *Blue All Around*. After you read, I will ask you what you understand about the book.

The teacher reads two pages of the text to the student, pointing to the words, to model the sentence pattern. In this conference, the teacher is looking for how the student reads the beginning consonant aloud and references the accompanying photos.

The student reads the text silently to herself.

Teacher: Follow the words on the page with your finger as you read to me.

Student: (The student tracks the words on the page with her finger as she reads aloud to the teacher.) That is a blue truck. That is a blue door. Door? (She looks at the teacher and asks if she pronounced *door* correctly). This is a blue motor…[cycle] (She giggles as she tries to decode "cycle" but is not able to do so.) That is a blue f..fl.. flower. That is a blue car.

Teacher smiles and uses non-verbal cues for encouragement.

The teacher asks the student a few comprehension questions and the student responds.

Figure 4.2 Sample reading conference

Comprehension questions	Student responses
Q1. What is this book about? What is the color?	(In Spanish) It has a lot of things that move. And everything is blue
Q2. Where is the truck? Where is the door? How do you know?	Because it has "truck" and "door" (Student points to the words *truck* and the *door*.)
Q3. What two things are similar? How are they similar?	Student points to the blue truck and the blue car. She says, "Truck and car."

Then, the teacher checks for specific skills for the level of the text she is using in the reading assessment. The teacher points to a list of consonants in the skill inventory, and the student says the sound for the consonant as the teacher takes notes in the skill inventory to assess accuracy. The teacher points to a set of high-frequency and sight words for that text level. The teacher asks the student to read the word and then define or translate the meaning.

Word	Student responses
is	is (in English)
this	"have/take" (in Spanish)
on	"for" (in Spanish

Teacher: You used picture clues to help you tell me this word. (Points to word). You gave me the beginning sound for the truck and door. When you know all the words, you will read more challenging texts. So practice reading at this text level on your own. Thank you! Good work! (Teacher gives the student a handshake.)

Figure 4.2 (Continued)

In this example, the student used Spanish when she wanted to express ideas she could not express in English. A reading assessment like this meets the specific needs of ELs by giving teachers information about a student's use of home language and its role in the student's reading practices. This is critical information teachers can use to assess comprehension.

Classroom Progress Monitoring Using English and Home Language Writing Data

In addition to reading instruction and practice in oral language production, the need for systematic, explicit instruction in specific writing components is imperative. Students must learn to encode English words; use simple, compound, and complex syntax to communicate ideas and relationships between concepts; connect ideas using transition words and discourse markers to develop and advance ideas; and learn conventions used in written English language. Moreover, they must learn to do this fluently to compose texts that express disciplinary and analytical thinking. As students develop oral language and learn to read increasingly complex academic texts, they require explicit instruction in language and literacy skills for writing.

Writing in a new language is a complex task and set of skills, with which ELs experience significant challenges (Knapp & Watkins, 2010; Hyland, 2003; Nesamalar et al., 2001). In the 2011 National Assessment of Educational Progress (NAEP) writing assessment, only 1% of 12th grade ELs performed at or above the proficient level compared with 27% for all students (NAEP, 2011). An unacceptable 80% of ELs scored below basic level! Corroborating the NAEP data, other studies in writing outcomes suggest that ELs need systematic, explicit instruction in writing even as they also engage in project-based teaching and learning cycles (Knapp & Watkins, 2010; Uccelli et al., 2012; Uccelli et al., 2015). For adolescent multilingual learners, the literacy education in their country of origin does not always emphasize the kind of disciplinary and analytical writing they are asked to do at the secondary level in the United States (Yip, 2016). Hence, they often benefit from explicit writing instruction in their home language and in English. For long-term ELs, the system has often failed to support them in developing academic writing skills in English or in their home language, so gathering information to better understand student progress is key to advancing their literacy skills.

A multilingual learner data framework is not complete without student writing composed in various academic subjects and includes writing in the student's home language when possible. English language proficiency assessments include a writing component but may not provide actionable information to teachers. As discussed in Chapter 2, teachers can collect student writing from content courses and analyze written work with a heuristic to monitor writing development as *they separately assess comprehension of content, highlighting the strengths of students' language practices and ideas expressed in home language.* Bridges to Academic Success (2019) developed with the

City University of New York a Newcomer Writing Rubric drawing on the 6+1 writing traits (Coe et al., 2011) that helps teachers evaluate language development traits such as sentence fluency separate from the grasp of ideas, which can also be expressed in home language in writing or verbally initially (See Table 4.3 for the ideas trait and Appendix C for the full rubric.)

As teachers review student writing against the traits in the rubric, they begin to develop a deeper understanding of what students are able to do with language in their writing. The rubric can also guide teachers in terms of which specific writing skills students are ready to learn next. Teachers can use the data with students in various ways, communicating the specific feedback to students through different formats or mechanisms. The teacher can keep track of the findings from the use of the rubric as a way of progress monitoring. Most important, teachers can provide feedback to students by honing in on no more than one or two traits for a student to reflect on so that students can monitor their own progress. See Table 4.4 for an example of feedback a teacher may give on an individual student's writing traits. Individual or peer writing conferences support this kind of monitoring and even if performed just a few times per year, can help teachers pinpoint meaningful and differentiated feedback to students.

This feedback is for a more advanced EL with intermediate language acquisition and output in writing. For a newcomer with developing home language and English writing skills, it is also possible to use visuals such as emojis to provide feedback and support verbal conferencing with the student. Students often appreciate the opportunity to receive acknowledgement of their ideas, whether in home language or English, and teachers report this can help build confidence in the new language.

Classroom Progress Monitoring for Social-Emotional Learning

Finally, schools can use SEL screeners as well as other ways of collecting data, including collaboration between counselors and teachers, to support learning and development of EL SEL skills targeted at specific competencies. Co-teachers can work together to support learning in specific sub-skills within the classroom as can teacher teams across classrooms. SEL strategies can be

Table 4.3 Newcomer writing rubric for clarity and development of ideas

Ideas: Does the writer clearly and appropriately communicate ideas relative to the prompt?					
	1 Attempted	2 Emerging	3 Developing	4 Consistent	5 Strong
Clarity and development	Attempted expression of ideas, but responses may be minimal or difficult to interpret	Expresses simple ideas with emerging clarity, but intended meaning is not fully expressed and/or may be confusing to readers; responses may be list-like or have minimal topic development	Simple ideas are generally clear, but concepts may not be fully developed or elaborated; some use of support and elaboration of ideas may be present, but the reader may have to fill in gaps in meaning	Consistent expression of simple ideas with some detail and specificity; topic development and support for ideas is often general rather than specific	Strong expression of simple ideas with detail and specificity; some complexity also present, but meaning may occasionally be obscured as more complex ideas are developed

(Bridges to Academic Success, 2019)

Table 4.4 Providing traits-based writing feedback to students

Trait	Strength	To Improve
Ideas score: 3	You give many examples of how people use power. *– Nasir, dad, yourself, people in Ghana*	Add more details to each example. *– Yes, Nasir travels to the United States for education. Now add more details. How does education give Nasir power?*
Word choice score: 3	You are trying to use academic words! *– education, solve your problems, disabled people*	As you read and speak more English, you will try to use more academic words in correct ways.

Table 4.5 SEL competencies assessment

1. Self-management To what degree was the student able to manage himself? Did s/he . . . • manage her/his emotions? • show self-discipline and motivation? • organize and plan?
2. Relationship skills To what degree was the student able to collaborate with others? Did s/he . . . • take on leadership roles? • interact with diverse groups? • support others?
3. Social awareness To what degree was the student able to empathize with others? Did s/he . . . • understand the perspectives of others? • show compassion for others? • express gratitude?
4. Responsible decision making To what degree was the student able to make responsible decisions about his behavior? Did s/he . . . • keep an open mind? • anticipate consequences? • reflect on his role in situations?
5. Self-awareness To what degree was the student able to understand himself? Did s/he . . . • identify her/his language and cultural assets? • examine prejudices? • have a growth mindset?

(Competencies from CASEL, 2019)

developed with existing curricula or integrated into classroom curricula to promote such learning alongside literacy exhibited in reading, writing, listening, and speaking. In Table 4.5, we share a tool to assess and progress monitor with a specific student mid-year adapted from CASEL competencies.

Bringing It All Together: Classroom Examples of Using Data to Design Classroom Instruction for Multilingual Learners

We now return to Katya's classroom from Chapter 3 to highlight ways that she makes an effort to integrate a multilingual learner data framework to design targeted instruction for ELs with a range of assets and needs. In Katya's lesson, the objective was to analyze the key events in the suffrage movement and the significance of the passing of the 19th amendment. The physical environment in her classroom included word walls, anchor charts translated in multiple languages for group routines such as partner work, and the protocol for the day's lesson, also translated into home languages.

She used a reading protocol that was differentiated based on data she collected on reading skills. She introduced an essential question to the class in English, Spanish, and Arabic on her SMART Board: *Why is voting important to democracy?* She prompted students to share a response. She introduced the 19th Amendment and key vocabulary. She used choral response and visuals to pre-teach target words before showing a video clip on the 19th Amendment and women's right to vote. She guided students through an initial "see-think-wonder" protocol in which they recorded their interpretation of what they saw and wrote down examples from the clip in home language using visuals to anchor their writing. She directed students to use sentence frames during the discussion protocol: "I see that women are talking about. . . ." "I think the next thing that will happen is. . . ." "I believe that voting is/is not important because. . . ." Students participated in discussion using their home language and English in preparation for reading the key text in the lesson.

Katya worked with a teaching assistant to differentiate groupings based on the state's language assessment and reading running records administered early in the year. She decided to group students who scored "entering" on the state assessment together for that day's lesson to provide reading instruction for that group. Many of the students were very new to English with limited literacy in their home language. She found a text that was accessible for her students, though it still provided challenges for her two students with limited and interrupted formal education (SLIFE). The teaching assistant worked with the rest of the class, primarily the emerging students, who used a more complex reading on the suffrage movement in three other groups. Katya guided two groups of students through a reading protocol that helped them annotate in their home language first. For the entering students, she used a teacher-made glossary for students to access key words with visuals for students to develop word recognition and familiarize themselves with their meanings. These decisions were made based on the teacher's evaluation of students' strengths and needs in literacy but also created spaces for students to engage in learning responsive to their needs.

Many additional examples from this classroom demonstrate that the targeted literacy instruction was also designed with inclusive methods in mind to ensure that students were supported in SEL as they learned to tackle literacy skills. In this classroom, students were taught to work together using a collaboration and discussion protocol, tools that integrate the SEL Domain of Relationship Skills and provide language for students that facilitate effective collaboration. Students negotiated their collaboration and peer work in both home language and English, depending on the activity. They engaged in partner talk about target words and were expected to create a definition of their own or write a sentence using the new word. Moreover, the student collaboration with peers moved students toward learner independence.

Specifically, the methods Katya used to scaffold the reading of complex English texts in the lesson shows just how much students must leverage social-emotional skills in order to tackle a cognitive task such as reading. In this classroom, students read leveled texts in English in order to engage with content and use thinking maps to guide their learning and make their thinking visible. The students filled out a sequence map to analyze the key events in order of their occurrence. This activity was accessible to entering EL students because they had 1) a partner to work with, or 2) for the students who need more guided practice, they work directly with the teacher. She used "hugs and pushes," a strategy to provide feedback to the group in a safe, constructive way. She provides feedback during individual conferencing to elicit goals from the students so they can better target the SEL domain of self-management and to help students become used to goal setting as a regular practice. The following day, Katya provided a mini-lesson on key language structures for this group to help them access the text while students who have more access to the language skills worked with a partner. In this way, students were slowly able to access the text and internalize the protocol they frequently use when reading texts. For the full protocol, please see Appendix C.

Throughout the lessons, Katya provided specific feedback on what the students did well and what they could improve in reading and writing using comprehensible language with visuals that support ELs at a variety of levels. Through this, the teacher builds community and individual relationships, partnerships that are critical because trust and risk taking are important to language learning and literacy development. Finally, building these relationships leads to managing conflict as a way to improve collaboration. For more strategies on integrating SEL into instruction and counselors as partners, please refer to Chapter 3.

The Power of Small-Group Interventions: Using Data to Design Targeted Tier 2 Instruction for ELs

In addition to the group learning happening independently of Katya in her classroom, in this scenario, she has designed targeted instruction for students based on their reading comprehension and reading running records. She scheduled reading conferences on a biweekly basis to check in with students and monitor their progress in reading. She used a writing rubric that helped her define student progress on a variety of domains and writing traits. She identified which skills the students needed to learn. For the students who needed more support, she planned a push-in intervention so that either she or her teaching assistant would support each student with Tier 2 language and content interventions in the classroom. In an inclusion classroom, this may also include a co-teacher. As a result of working with students on day 1, Katya created a mini-lesson on English language skills for day 2 with a small group of students struggling with accessing the more basic text.

This targeted instruction for a small group can be done both inside the Tier 1 regularly scheduled "core" instruction, as part of a pullout group, or after school. It is most effective when some Tier 2 instruction is maximized during classroom instruction; otherwise, we see students in Tier 1 classrooms who are unable to access the instruction and materials on an everyday basis. Writing and reading conferences performed either with individual students or peer groups can support teachers in providing ongoing, timely feedback that also helps teach students how to self-evaluate their own work as well as that of others. Tier 2 is also an effective way to practice specific social skills; for example, a teacher can more closely monitor how the group is working together and provide more scaffolds if required. Are there sources of conflict that need to be addressed? If the teacher has the capacity to work with a small Tier 2 group regularly focused on specific instructional and/or SEL skills, this can accelerate their progress more effectively.

Tier 3 Interventions for ELs: How Do We Differentiate a Disability From a Language Need?

One frequent pitfall that schools face is determining when and what type of intensive instruction is needed, particularly when it comes to sussing out a student's needs when they have a disability versus when they are developing new language skills. First, schools are often not equipped to diagnose and differentiate language needs in teams. As a result, the complex nuanced questions that involve differentiating disability from language supports result in confusion and interventions that do not match the student's needs. Often, ELs are thus *both over- and under*referred for special education services (Losen, 2014). For students who are dual identified, content teachers are not adequately trained to support them, and they may not always have a partnership with a special educator or language teacher with whom they can collaborate and design the right interventions and scaffolds for the student. Educators need ongoing professional learning and collaboration with other educators to understand the struggles students face when learning a new language and the basic signs of most frequently identified learning disabilities, which would lead to a more equitable referral process. Although we delve into some examples of this, see Collier (2011) and Hamayan et al. (2013) for a more in-depth look at how to refine team interventions to address both language and learning disability.

In some districts, Tier 3 instruction is considered special education. For multilingual learners, the road to pinpointing specific learning issues is more complex as it can be challenging to differentiate between the need for special education services and language remediation. As a result, Tier 3 status may indicate either one and does not necessarily indicate the need for a referral. What it does indicate at the school level is that differentiated Tier 1 and 2 instructional methods are still insufficient for some students to make progress, and a more rigorous and targeted approach is needed. Tier 3 status may provide more time for a qualified teacher to work with the student one on one to better understand where the gaps are and how to best support a student in the area of struggle in a particular class. Students can also be evaluated using SEL indicators (provided in Chapter 3), since academic challenges may arise not only to problems with literacy skills but also because students may need social-emotional strategies to support their academic learning.

Consider Makini's classroom. As discussed in Chapter 3, she worked in a specialized district for students with disabilities and was the ENL teacher in charge of intake for ELs, administering and monitoring instruction. Even in a district with highly specialized instruction with teachers who are used to working with and trained in monitoring special needs, there are challenges to achieving individualized instruction, particularly in staffing and the ability to carve out time to meet with individual students on a regular basis. As a result, grouping students becomes crucial for effective tiered instruction. Makini grouped students in her class with specific language and special needs to be able to better serve them with specific literacy programs used in her school. Even paired or small grouping with distinct clarity in learning targets can produce great results for students. Here is the story of Makini and her 13-year-old EL student with autism who was able to receive additional small group instruction during the COVID-19 pandemic:

> Obviously, all kids benefit from 1:1 [instruction]! However, targeted group work can help, especially when there are other adults in the room. We would sing this song every week in Saturday school together, but one student was always quiet. All of a sudden one day, I heard this voice sing; it was her! She had found her voice and was able to participate. She has grown so much during the pandemic. She went from not completing a sentence or paragraph in March to writing a three-paragraph essay in October. Now she is more vocal about her needs and advocates for herself.

In addition to helping this student feel more successful in her writing, Makini's feedback also supported her SEL and ability to self-advocate, a trait of the CASEL competency of self-awareness. Targeted group work helped the student improve her writing skills since she had the extra support. Moreover, Makini's encouragement during the group sessions supported the student to become more comfortable taking risks. Particularly for ELs, for whom language learning can be an additional barrier to accessing curriculum, one-to-one instruction and small group work make a big difference, especially if strategically planned over time with progress monitoring.

School-wide Planning for Language, Literacy, and SEL

While the description of these teachers' classrooms may seem like unique examples, in schools that work toward coherence and alignment in instructional and literacy strategies, shared practices are commonplace. These school communities hone in on a small set of strategies they believe address the specific skills students are ready to learn and have a shared commitment to implementing practices consistently across classrooms and to reflecting on the impact of these practices on student learning. This helps school communities to develop a common language and shared understanding about which practices are considered high-impact for their multilingual learners, co-created in agreement among educators and incorporating teacher expertise. At one urban elementary school, the 5th grade school team integrated their focus on equity by inviting all teachers to inventory strategies they found would help their multilingual students be more successful. Table 4.6 shows what this community determined to be "high-impact instructional strategies" they were committed to using to support multilingual learners across content areas.

The creation of this list suggests that instructional teams may benefit from creating an "instructional playbook," a resource that supports successful implementation of high-impact teaching strategies that can be used by teacher teams as well as by coaches who design professional learning or who support individual teachers (Knight et al., 2020). As a team collaborates to create their own collective instructional toolbox, they establish a community of practice and learning. Teacher teams discuss practices they feel can be realistically integrated into their practice to serve multilingual learners and focus on using and getting good at implementing a relatively small set of high-impact teaching strategies. Even when teachers might not always understand or have not yet had extensive training in the science of language or reading development, the instructional playbook can go a long way in offering teachers a way to learn new practices in a way that feels integrated in their work. Once an instructional playbook is written, it serves as a professional development tool and resource that can be adjusted as the team learns about what works with their students or induct a new teacher into the practices that are consistently used in a school community.

Table 4.6 Team artifact: Classroom strategies for differentiating instruction by content, process, or product

For all learners struggling to comprehend text	Use of the following classroom tools: • Graphic organizers • Anchor charts • 1:1 conferencing • Sentence starters • Model texts • Mentor texts • Visible essential questions • Small group instruction • Frequent check-ins
For ELs in general	• Home language support (including translated texts) • Videos and visuals related to the topic • Opportunities for discussions to share what they understand and don't understand • Clear, concise rubric or checklist • Writing conferences • Teacher model and student model work
For emerging EL writers	• Labeling images, infographics, visuals, and/or graphs or charts related to story chapters • Sorting or identifying: fragment (phrase) vs. sentence exercises to support reading comprehension • Retelling the story or chapter using visuals and native language • Using transition or sequence words to retell chapter or story • Identifying theme or lesson using abstract nouns (i.e., fear, friendship, love) • Identifying words or phrases that are repeated • Identifying adjectives and verbs that describe how a character feels or what a character does • Describing how a character responds to a challenge using native language or pictures • Matching character trait word to phrases that exemplify the trait • Matching protagonist's character trait to specific examples or quotes from the book • Writing topic sentences such as: "The character [character name] shows that he/she is . . . in many ways." • Writing supporting details from the text such as: "One example of [character name] is when . . ." using pre-selected phrases and words. • Writing concluding sentences such as: "In conclusion, [character name] shows that he/she is . . . in many ways." • Sorting pre-selected information (words and phrases) into graphic organizers • Matching pre-selected supporting reasons to pre-selected claims • Using home language support for new vocabulary words and ideas • Clozing sentences to support use of Tier 1 and 2 vocabulary words and ideas

For developing EL writers	• Note-taking graphic organizers • Identifying adjectives and verbs that describe how a character feels or what a character does • Describing how a character responds to a challenge (cause/effect) • Using transition words and phrases to describe effect (i.e., thus, therefore, one consequence, however, nonetheless) • Writing topic sentences that restate prompt [In the story . . ., the author develops the theme of . . . in many ways/the character [character name] shows that he/she is . . . in many ways] • Writing supporting details from the text ["One example of this theme is when . . ."/"One example of [character name]'s [trait] is when . . ."] • Identifying theme using repeated words, phrases, or ideas in the text • Writing simple sentences for conclusion "In conclusion, . . ." • Writing planning template (topic sentence, three details, concluding sentence) • Clozing sentences for Tier 2 and 3 vocabulary words/ideas
For advanced EL writers	• Note-taking graphic organizers to note examples of a theme developed throughout the book • Note-taking graphic organizers to note examples of a character trait developed throughout the book • Graphic organizers to support analysis of character motives • Writing planning template (RACE: restate the answer, answer the question, cite, explain the answer) • Sentence stems • Writing planning template (claim or topic sentence, details, analysis, concluding sentence) • Writing activities with a focus on expanded sentences, complex sentences, use of conjunctions, use of appositive, subordinating conjunction, adding voice (statement, question, command, exclamation)

Developing a Multilingual Learner Data Action Plan

Schools that leverage a multilingual learner data framework in their classroom core instruction get better at knowing the strengths and needs of the students in their community. As schools engage in such efforts, they expand and deepen their understanding of students, their cultures, and communities and improve how they integrate support across classrooms. A multilingual learner data framework guides decision making in how to

- ◆ Use a variety of screeners early in the year to assess home language literacy in a variety of content areas, describe educational background and history, and set a baseline for SEL skills.
- ◆ Group students for collaboration and relationship building.
- ◆ Promote student self-management and self-regulation through routines that are explicitly taught and monitored.
- ◆ Vary scaffolding appropriately when students interact with a text set.
- ◆ Determine what type of scaffolding is needed based on the students' areas of need in relation to the components of reading.
- ◆ Identify specific learning targets for explicit instruction to small groups.
- ◆ Determine the type of home language supports to use and leverage home language as a cognitive tool for reading, writing, and learning.
- ◆ Design formative assessments to assess reading comprehension and progress in writing.
- ◆ Select literacy routines that target the development of specific components of reading.
- ◆ Provide feedback on writing traits such as 6+1, state rubrics, other language assessments.
- ◆ Determine Tier 1, 2, and 3 vocabulary to teach to different groups of students along the language and literacy continuum.

A school cannot and should not initiate the implementation of all the types of assessments in the multilingual learner data framework at once. Instead, schools should consider what questions they are trying to answer about their students and use that line of inquiry to further implement the use of tiered assessments as the expertise of practitioners evolve and arise. Specific data need to be collected by designated educators, entered consistently into a data tracking system, and incorporated into team meeting agendas. EL practitioners are a vital resource for instructional teams as they learn to analyze the data. Using the data within interconnected and established processes increases alignment and coherence in the support provided to students not just in an intervention space but also in a sustained manner across classrooms and school activities. School communities can implement a multilingual learner data framework based on student population, staff expertise, and resource allocation. Table 4.7 provides a loose roadmap for planning and decision making for a school to solidify organizational structures, resources, and leverage data they have collected to improve their system for multilingual learner success.

A multilingual learner data framework requires strategic planning to operationalize. No school takes on the analysis of multiple data sources at once because practitioners often need an initial period of time to develop assessment literacy first. The other chapters in this book speak to the other systems criteria needed for the use of data to be effective: teacher teaming to help build knowledge and capacity and create local solutions and understandings of various forms of data (Chapter 2) and leadership practices to implement a strategic plan over a period of time to develop the organization's resilience and interconnectedness for doing this type of work (Chapter 5). We also know that this work cannot be done without systematic social-emotional support to students (Chapters 3). The examples in this chapter highlight the need for schools to coordinate professional learning and collaboration among practitioners in order for effective literacy and SEL practices to be embedded meaningfully in a school and how teachers use progress monitoring data to make strategic decisions and address equity or disproportionality in everyday classroom practice. As schools create organization-wide structures that are interconnected, teachers learn how to assess literacy, deepening their desire to understand what their students need and a hunger for concrete strategies to help students grow. It becomes a virtuous cycle that improves the organization's capacity to serve multilingual learners.

Table 4.7 Multilingual learner data action plan

	Key Actions	Considerations
Year 1	• Establish a purpose for using data (reading, writing, speaking, listening, SEL). • Inventory existing data system – identify strengths and gaps. • Determine what data to collect. • Develop data and assessment literacy among school staff around multiple components. • Ensure that team structures are put in place to analyze data and undergo inquiry and child study practices (collaborative team teachers, grade-level teams, interdisciplinary teams).	• What data sources are you currently using? Is this the right data source? If so, how do you use it, and do you need to make any changes in the way sources are used? • What data sources do you think you need but are not currently using? • What would it take to gather and organize these data? • What do you want to learn from these data? • What is the implementation plan for collecting, tracking, extracting, and interpreting these data with stakeholders at your school? • Which data sources will help us serve the learning objectives of the practitioners (not the students)? • When will instructional or interdisciplinary teams gather to evaluate the impact of those strategies?
Year 2	• Routinize and systematize data collection processes. • Improve the technical aspects of data systems to facilitate easy access to information and build practitioner understanding of how to interpret the data. • Bridge the data/practice divide by focusing on using the interpretation of data to inform practice. • Monitor progress of interventions and evaluate the impact of strategies. • Monitor team development and build shared leadership among facilitators.	• What do school staff need to learn how to do and assess in order to build their capacity to assess the strengths and needs of multilingual learners? • Who are the key stakeholders who are responsible for data collection, and who do they need to collaborate with? • What tools or protocols build the knowledge of school staff to understand what the data are telling them about their multilingual learners? • What technical capabilities are needed to facilitate easy entry and access of data? • How will classroom teachers and counselors learn how to access, interpret, and use the data? • How will instructional teams translate their interpretations to develop aligned strategies that support students? • How will instructional teams interpret collected data and evaluate the impact of implemented strategies on stated goals for multilingual learners? • How will instructional teams measure the impact of their strategies, quantitatively or qualitative?

| Year 3 | • Adjust and codify a long-term data framework.
• Determine specific data to track within a school year that are aligned to school-wide goals and theory of change for multilingual learners.
• Implement strategies aligned to theory of change and determine timeline for collecting data based on those strategies.
• Evaluate the impact of implemented strategies based on data collected.
• Decide on a timeline to evaluate and make adjustments to the data framework as the system and the needs of students changes over time. | • What is our theory of change to improve outcomes for multilingual learners?
• Which assessments will best help us understand the efficacy of this theory of change?
• Which specific data points will help us understand the impact of implemented strategies?
• How do we need to adjust our instructional and systems practices to support multilingual learners? |

References

Abedi, J. (2006). Psychometric issues in the ELL assessment and special education eligibility. *Teachers College Record*, *108*(11), 2282–2303.

Benson, T. A., & Fiarman, S. E. (2020). *Unconscious bias in schools: A developmental approach to racism*. Harvard Education Press.

Bridges to Academic Success. (2019). *Newcomer writing rubric*. City University of New York.

Bridges to Academic Success. (n.d.). *[School Training Organization]*. City University of New York. https://bridges-sifeproject.com/.

Coe, M., Hanita, M., Nishioka, V., & Smiley, R. (2011). *An investigation of the impact of the 6+1 trait writing model on grade 5 student writing achievement* (NCEE 2012–4010). National Center for Education Evaluation and Regional Assistance, Institute of Education Sciences, U.S. Department of Education. https://ies.ed.gov/ncee/edlabs/regions/northwest/pdf/REL_20124010.pdf

Collaborative for Academic, Social, and Emotional Learning (CASEL). 2019. *SEL Assessment Guide*. https://measuringsel.casel.org/access-assessment-guide/

Collier, C.-C. (2011). *Seven steps to separating difference from disability*. Corwin.

Durlak, J. A., Domitrovich, C. E., Weissberg, R. P., & Gullotta, T. P. (Eds.). (2015). *Handbook of social and emotional learning: Research and practice*. The Guilford Press.

Fountas, I. C., & Pinnell, G. S. (1996). *Guided reading: good first teaching for all children*. Heinemann.

Hamayan, E. V., Marler, B., Lopez, C. S., & Damico, J. (2013). *Special education considerations for English language learners: Delivering a continuum of services*. Caslon Publishing.

Hawn Nelson, A., Jenkins, D., Zanti, S., Katz, M., Berkowitz, E., et al. (2020). *A toolkit for centering racial equity throughout data integration*. Actionable Intelligence for Social Policy, University of Pennsylvania.

Hileman, J., & Cline, G. Z. (2014). *IRLA: Independent reading level assessment framework* [Measurement instrument]. American Reading Company.

Hochman, J. C., & Wexler, N. (2017). *The writing revolution: A guide to advancing thinking through writing in all subjects and grades*. John Wiley & Sons.

Hopkins, M., Thompson, K. D., Linquanti, R., Hakuta, K., & August, D. (2013). Fully accounting for English learner performance: A key issue in ESEA reauthorization. *Educational Researcher*, *42*(2), 101–108.

Hyland, K. (2003). *Second language writing*. Cambridge University Press. http://doi.org/10.1017/CBO9780511667251

Knapp, P., & Watkins, M. (2010). *Genre, text, grammar: Technologies for teaching and assessing writing*. University of New South Wales Press.

Knight, J., Hoffman, A., Harris, M., & Thomas, S. (2020). *The instructional playbook: The missing link for translating research into practice*. ASCD & One Fine Bird Press.

LeBuffe, P. A., & Naglieri, J. A. (1998). *The Devereux early childhood assessment*. Kaplan.

LeBuffe, P. A., Shapiro, V. B., & Naglieri, J. A. (2009). *Devereux student strengths assessment (DESSA)*. Kaplan.

Linquanti, R. (2001). *The redesignation dilemma: Challenges and choices in fostering meaningful accountability for English learners* (Policy Report 2001–1). University of California Linguistic Minority Research Institute.

Losen, D. J. (Ed.). (2014). *Closing the school discipline gap: Equitable remedies for excessive exclusion*. Teachers College Press.

Martohardjono, G. (2015). *NYSED Multilingual Literacy SIFE Screener* [Measurement instrument]. New York State Education Department, Office of Bilingual Education and World Languages. http://mls.slalab.org

Merrell, K. W. (n.d.). *SEARS: Social Emotional Assets and Resilience Scales™* [Measurement Instrument]. Par, Inc.

National Assessment of Educational Progress (NAEP). (2011). *Grade 12 national results. U.S. department of education, institute of education sciences, national center for education statistics*. www.nationsreportcard.gov/writing_2011/g12_national.aspx?subtab_id=Tab_8&tab_id=tab2#chart

Nesamalar, C., Saratha, S., & Teh, S. (2001). *ELT methodology: Principles and practice*. Penerbit Fajar Bakti.

Northwest Evaluation Association (NWEA). (2000). *Map growth* [Measurement Instrument]. Northwest Evaluation Association.

NYSED. (n.d.). *New York State English as a Second Language Achievement Test (NYSESLAT)* [Measurement Instrument]. New York State Department of Education.

NYSED. (n.d.). *New York State Identification Test for English Language Learners (NYSITELL)* [Measurement Instrument]. New York State Department of Education.

Renaissance. (2015). *STAR reading assessment in Spanish* [Measurement instrument]. Renaissance.

Sanchez, L. M., Hileman, J., & Cline, G. Z. (2013). *Estructura para la evaluación del nivel independiente de lectura* [Measurement instrument]. American Reading Company.

School Reform Initiative. (2021). *ATLAS protocol.* www.school reforminitiative.org/download/atlas-looking-at-data/

Uccelli, P., Barr, C., Dobbs, C., Galloway, E., Meneses, A., & Sánchez, E. (2015). Core academic language skills: An expanded operational construct and a novel instrument to chart school-relevant language proficiency in preadolescent and adolescent learners. *Applied Psycholinguistics, 36*(5), 1077–1109. https://doi.org/10.1017/S014271641400006X

Uccelli, P., Dobbs, C. L., & Scott, J. (2012). Mastering academic language: Organization and stance in the persuasive writing of high school students. *Written Communication, 30*(1), 36–62.

Umansky, I., & Dumont, H. (2019). *English learner labeling: How English learner status shapes teacher perceptions of student skills & the moderating role of bilingual instructional settings* (EdWorkingPaper: 19–94). Annenberg Institute at Brown University. www.edworkingpapers.com/ai19-94

WIDA. (n.d.). *WIDA screener* [Measurement Instrument]. Wisconsin Center for Education Research.

WIDA Consortium. (2013). *Culturally and linguistically responsive RtI planning form.* https://morethanenglish.edublogs.org/files/2013/09/RtI2-Planning-Form-for-ELLs-WIDA-1y4ki5q.pdf

Woodcock, R. W., Alvarado, C. G., & Ruef, M. (2017). *Woodcock-Muñoz language survey* [Measurement instrument]. Riverside. www.txautism.net/evaluations/woodcock-mu%C3%B1oz-language-survey-third-edition

Yip, J. (2016). *Educational histories of newcomer immigrant youth: From countries of origin to the United States.* CUNY Academic Works. http://academicworks.cuny.edu/gc_etds/1616

5

Leading School Improvement for Multilingual Learners

This chapter is about leading school improvement that helps multilingual learners thrive in school. It is about the hard choices and critical decisions leaders make in their context and how leadership practice makes the difference in transforming school communities to reach their highest aspirations for their multilingual learners. Systems criteria 4 is *deepen leadership practice and organizational learning for school improvement*.

To improve schools for multilingual learners, the role of the school leader is often to bring together elements of the system in particular ways that respond to the needs of their contexts, to build capacity through sustainable structures, to coordinate transfer of information, to facilitate collective problem solving, and to align key actions and strategies with the school community's stated beliefs and values. Such a project involves both technical challenges (developing expertise and practical considerations) as well as adaptive challenges, such as changing mindsets and beliefs and engaging stakeholders in collective decision making (Heifetz et al., 2009).

During this process of change, school organizations inevitably experience resistance, a sense of loss of what used to be, unfamiliarity with new policies, lack of agreement on key decisions affecting various stakeholders, or even a lack of good will due to the mishandling of decision-making

DOI: 10.4324/9781003123392-5

processes. Often the teaching English to speakers of other languages (TESOL), literacy, or special education staff feel they are battling existing systems and culture as they advocate for change, even as general education and content teachers face enormous pressure and unrealistic demands with limited resources. It is when school leaders set a path forward and direct existing systems and structures to focus on requisite priorities that these tensions turn into opportunities to truly serve all students.

Furthermore, when leaders organize for student achievement and equity for multilingual learners, they simultaneously lead system level changes that improve the school organization as a whole and empower their staff to address the needs of all students. This is not a commonly held belief, but it is one that makes a difference. A focus on English learners (ELs) requires schools to coalesce around core practices in curriculum planning, instruction, school culture, and programming. Equity for multilingual learners means taking an anti-racist stance in practice; implementing system-level changes in budget and staffing; and pushing for shifts in beliefs, values, and mindsets. The resulting innovations benefit other students who have historically been marginalized by inequitable school systems and structures: students with disabilities, students with interrupted schooling, and culturally and linguistically diverse students who have not been provided effective literacy education.

Leadership Practice for Multilingual Learner Success

The systems criteria we have discussed in previous chapters do not come about organically. They are direct results of intentional leadership practices and decisions that prioritize adult development, the creation of systems and structures aligned with a school's vision and purpose, collaborative structures that facilitate organizational learning and problem solving, and an asset-based orientation toward multilingual learners. Table 5.1 outlines the key roles that leaders play in defining, designing, and sustaining each criteria in the school organization.

Table 5.1 The role of school leaders in promoting systemwide learning for ELs

Systems Criteria	Role of School Leaders
#1 Team learning (Chapter 2)	• Define the goal and purpose of team collaboration. • Provide direction and feedback on team structures and routines. • Monitor the development and efficacy of teams. • Provide leadership development and support for team leaders to effectively lead teams and facilitate meetings.
#2 School-wide integrative practices for SEL and academic instruction (Chapter 3)	• Articulate an anti-racist and equity-focused vision for the culture and climate in the school that is inclusive of multilingual learners. • Create ongoing opportunities for pedagogical and counseling staff to collaborate. • Secure resources that help develop the expertise and knowledge of all staff to support SEL and rigorous and accessible pedagogy.
#3 Culturally and linguistically responsive data practices to learn about students and improve the system by exposing inequity (Chapter 4)	• Define the purpose of using data in the school community and how the data are relevant to classroom instruction and aligned with school goals. • Guide the development and monitor the progress of the implementation of a Multilingual Learner Data framework to improve instruction and SEL. • Delegate the responsibilities of collecting, interpreting, and decision making in response to data. • Create systems that support data collection aligned with articulated goals.

In this chapter, we present leadership vignettes of four administrators in varying contexts, based on interviews and document analysis. We showcase how leaders have come to understand the needs of their school organization, how they addressed obstacles as they worked to improve outcomes for ELs, how they built successful school environments for ELs, and what they learned along the way in their leadership experience. Their stories show how leaders get ahead of the change process and ensure there is a shared understanding of the school's vision, purpose, and goals for ELs, as they establish structures for shared decision making and problem solving as needs arise and communicate to school staff how they will be supported. Their stories highlight essential practices for leadership and organizational learning that lead to multilingual learner success. Each vignette is followed by a set of discussion questions to promote analysis of leadership practice using a case study approach. We envision the vignettes to be read and used as entry points for discussion among school leaders and administrators. As you review each one, analyze the central problem in each situation, consider what you would do and what questions you would consider if you were in the leader's shoes, and use the case to reflect on and hone your own approach to leadership and problem solving. We have also provided additional case studies to use in professional learning in Appendix D.

Leadership Vignette: Building Relationships in School Communities

When Charlene Nieves started her role as assistant principal (AP), she was used to working alone in isolation. At a large public high school of 2000 students in Queens, Newtown High School had a transitional bilingual education program for their over 1500 ELs. After working as a teacher for 10 years, Charlene realized that things had to change in order to more effectively serve their ELs. One of the first things she realized needed to change was the way her teachers made decisions and solved problems in their work. She saw a significant need for collaboration:

> When I started teaching, I was by myself. Now I see it's not me alone; it's a team. . . . As a teacher, I was more isolated. If I had a question or problem, I went to my AP. Now if my teachers have a problem, they go to their team.

Charlene assigned teachers to work in pairs to plan together and write lessons. Eventually, this practice led to structured small learning communities for teacher teams. Teams met regularly in 45-minute blocks. They discussed student work and shared information about the needs of their students together and they analyzed data to inform instruction. By creating the time and space, as well as the purpose, for team collaboration, Charlene established a culture for her teachers:

> Even to this day, if I have something others can use, I share it and tell others to make it their own. I want to make sure that others have the resources and they are not alone. I know how it is to be alone; that to me was the biggest change.

Charlene noticed that the shift to increased collaboration also had an impact on students: "It also transfers to the students; they work together and do group work. They are also part of a team."

Initially, teachers engaged in a practice to learn how to differentiate for the students. Teachers chose a focus group of two top students, two middle students, and two lower level students in language development. They shadowed them throughout a school day in each of their classes to observe what helped them thrive and where they struggled. They also tracked their assessment data throughout the year. Based on that exercise, the teachers looked at trends and information about the different levels of students to help inform classroom instruction. Charlene said, "I was trying to make the department more coherent so that teachers have consistency and that the skills and strategies they use are similar."

By establishing routines and ways of looking at data, this AP built the team's ability to use information they learned about students and to develop shared practices across their classrooms. Not surprisingly, this led to other implications for curriculum and instruction. Before to these teaming practices were implemented, class content was designed in very different ways by addressing a variety of standards across the various classrooms. After Charlene established the purpose and practices of the team, the curriculum and instruction moved increasingly toward internal coherence, requiring alignment in both standards and instructional goals across the classrooms. The lessons were similar in content and design. If the students transferred to a different class, the families were assured that their children would be engaging with the same material and same kinds of support. This helped manage alignment of instruction across classrooms and coherence among grade teams as well as with vertical alignment in terms of content and language objectives.

The team's internal organizational structure and culture was situated within the overall welcoming environment and consistent community-building opportunities that the school prioritized for ELs. Charlene believes her teachers' compassion and commitment to serving the student population were key:

> Since I come from a background where my grandparents and parents came here and didn't speak the language, it also helps me better understand my students. Having teachers and staff who care is really important. One of the things that has helped me push for ELs is that our building has mostly former ELs or ELs. [For example,] with the students with interrupted or inconsistent formal schooling (SIFE) program, originally the principal wasn't on board; what got him on board was to remind him that all students in school were once ELs. It is who we are as a building.

Alongside her teacher leaders, Charlene helped facilitate many kinds of family engagement and social activities for students. For example, the department created clubs that bring together the students around ethnicity, including those for Filipino, Bengali, and Dominican students. Former ELs join with current ELs to mingle and get to know one another. Charlene explained that students often come back to the program after they are no longer ELs and are mainstreamed. In this way, students have a place and teachers who know them well and can come back and check in. They also develop relationships with students they may not have otherwise. In addition to clubs, the department offered an art program and a media program in the summer. The teachers recruited ELs with over 100 students who were able to do art, create multimedia, write, and perform in front of other people, which can be very difficult for beginner ELs. Teachers created an environment where students could speak in their home language if they didn't feel comfortable with English. The program grew each year in the number of students served (until pausing for COVID).

For families, the department hosted regular dinners before COVID for parents and families, ensuring that they played a role in the school and their child's education.

> Often immigrant families don't participate, and we invited them and made sure they did. Even now in COVID, we do Zoom parent meetings with students and parents to build connections and conversations happening with teachers, parents, and children. With high school, it can be hard to get parents involved. If you have the teachers who are constantly checking in with the student, the parent will be more involved at times.

Using home language and either knowing or being willing to learn about other cultures was an integral part of leadership. Charlene said, "I can't speak fluent Spanish, but I try. I'm warm and welcoming and let them know they should come to my office. [You have to show] that side of you, that you care about anyone who comes into the building." Charlene's story highlights how integrating families into the life of the school helped create and sustain connections, communication, and collaboration between the school and the larger community regarding the well-being of each student and the success of school programs. The intentional opportunities Charlene and her team created regularly to deepen teacher and counselor partnership with families and caregivers is a part of what made the academic program successful.

Ultimately, Charlene's greatest strength in her efforts as a leader for multilingual learners and their teachers is serving as a teambuilder, a support system, and a connector. "Being available, being a listener is important and just making sure that the teachers have the available resources to be successful." Charlene's success in developing the EL program within her school was rooted in her ability to systematically build the structures for collaboration and relationship building not just between teachers but also among students and families, over time and year after year. These relationships became the heart of what makes her programs come to life, not only for students with limited and interrupted formal education but also for all multilingual learners in her building.

Discussion Questions

- ◆ What are some key actions this leader used to establish ongoing community building among stakeholders in her school?
- ◆ What are some continued challenges this leader might be facing, and how might she leverage the relationship-building she has established to address these challenges?
- ◆ How do you use relationship building to improve your school context for multilingual learners?

Leadership Vignette: Integrating SEL Through Strategic Staffing and Roles

In Chapter 3, we described a powerful example of a team meeting that showcased the close-knit collaboration between school counselors and teachers to provide holistic support to students and families. This team is also described in detail by Auslander (2018). This leadership vignette identifies the elements established by design to create a powerful integration of social-emotional learning (SEL) and academic support. The AP at a school for newcomers, who we will call Natalia Hernandez, had a unique background as a social worker, which influenced her approach to leading her school, first as the AP with the founding principal and now in her role as the principal. Natalia brought her experience from working in hospitals to the vision of how her school would serve the needs of her students:

> In a hospital setting, I was a social worker, but I didn't work on my own. I was part of the team of people that were included. We would include the HIV counselor, the nurse practitioner, the physician, the doctor, the lab, the person doing the non-stress tests, the clinicians, everybody. If I'm going to discharge a patient from the floor,

> we are working together to cover all these pieces. . . .
> That kind of model needs to happen in a school because
> we're dealing with the whole child. That's the vision or
> the philosophy around that and why this space functions
> somehow the way it does.

It is on this fundamental understanding of the teaming required
to support students – leveraging a network of adults who care
and deeply understand their students' needs – that Natalia
based her school's counseling program. With the right team and
the right structures, her school has served countless newcomer
immigrant youth, helping them to surmount extremely difficult
personal and social challenges.

Natalia and the school prioritized hiring not only the right
teachers but also counselors. Hiring was always done through collective decision making, and the school's leadership emphasized
to the hiring committees the kinds of skills that were needed to
support their unique population. The hiring processes involved
evaluating each candidate's experience working with immigrant
youth, and the committees actively pursued counselors with
expertise in trauma-informed practices. As a result of this practice, every staff member was not only knowledgeable about but
also empathetic toward the general needs of multilingual learners.
Natalia said: "We do hire very highly qualified clinical staff. I vet my
social workers. They can function in solo practice on their own and
can handle tough situations. That's how we kind of choose them.
We have a lot of opportunities to build confidence in them." Hiring
and intentional staffing was a key step in getting the right people
who understood the population and serving them in a complex
environment. The needs of the students inside and outside school
walls were always a priority. The school often leveraged their
partnership with social work university programs who trained
interns to provide a greater range of adult support to students.
With the right hiring processes in place, a leader could staff her
counseling positions with the right people and then largely step
out of the way to let those experts do their jobs. The counseling
team had autonomy in utilizing different approaches to support
students, such as individual and group counseling sessions based

on students with similar experiences. Yet even the talented counseling staff never worked alone.

Since the culture of collaboration in the school was strong, counselors and social workers, even social work interns, were regarded as necessary members of the instructional team. Teachers relied on the expertise of the counseling staff to help them understand students in a way that they were not trained to as pedagogues. Without this trust and deference to the expertise of the counselors, teachers could easily allow their decisions to be shaped by implicit bias rather than evidence of student's social and emotional development. At this school, the leader worked with her staff to set up systems for counselors, social workers, and teachers to collaborate regularly. Every meeting involved discussion of a student's social and emotional well-being. Conversations in the hallway among school staff often centered on the immediate and often urgent needs faced by newcomer immigrant youth.

Instructional teams met weekly with a designated member of the counseling team to discuss various ways to conduct outreach to families as student needs arose; they engaged in problem solving together when students were having particular challenges. The ability for the team to meet with counselors on a regular basis and the selected personnel on each team had implications for school schedules. Natalia emphasized that having flexibility as a leader and allowing the shift of resources was a key element making it all work. The strategic allocation of resources, primarily human capital and budget, created the school structures dedicated to collaboration and the culture of social-emotional support to thrive.

In this particular school, the roles of various staff members in coordinating social-emotional support were clear. Each student had one advisor who met with students through their advisory system multiple times a week, whose job it was to ensure the students' overall needs were met and help communicate information to other teachers and advocate for the student. The teams discussed issues related to particular students and established an understanding of which situations required the counseling team to play a greater role alongside instructional interventions. The team shared norms for engaging in conversations about students. The discourse was asset based, solutions focused, and authentic, giving room for the humanizing nature of youth development and social justice efforts.

In observing the teacher teams, teachers would intentionally bring in those who had deeper knowledge of a particular student's issues or had close bonds with them to help troubleshoot and identify strategies to support an individual student. This included paraprofessionals and special education teachers but also operations and school support staff. This meant that all staff, even if their job was to inventory the supply closet, knew that they had a hand in contributing to the community to support students. They also knew which family members to reach to communicate about a student's needs, with the immediate parent not always being available. This school provides an example of how to redefine the traditional role of support staff to include roles and responsibilities that support the larger goals of the community.

Discussion Questions

♦ Which practices related to staffing and role assignment in this leadership vignette are useful to your own school or district context?
♦ What are some continued challenges you see present in this leadership vignette that the leader would have to address?
♦ How is your own school context different or similar to this leadership vignette?
♦ Is there a strategic shift in resources that would allow your school to build a stronger community?

Leadership Vignette: Establishing a Vision and Infrastructure for Bilingual Program Development

District leader Sofia Lopez has been the bilingual and ENL education coordinator of a suburban district for the past 14 years and was a teacher for ten years prior. This district serves approximately 1,200 ELs, who make up about 20% of the student population. Almost 40% of the families in the district speak a language other than English, predominantly Spanish. One of the challenges in her leadership role has been to reshape the perception of bilingual education and learning. Sofia had a vision for bilingual education in her district and understood that making that vision a reality involved shifting beliefs and mindsets:

> We have a big problem in this country that learning two languages is not considered a strength. My goal is to create as many opportunities as possible to continue to build both languages for all students. It is important that we build a generation that perceives bilingualism as an asset, and this is often done one kid at a time. It is only through experiencing it that you can really believe this, which will create bilingualism for everyone.

As Sofia made structural changes to the programs in her district, she saw shifts in perceptions as well:

> When we first started, this district had a more multilingual population. We didn't have bilingual classes, but there was a big resistance to teaching home language arts (HLA) in Spanish. Originally, it was taught only to SLIFE students. It took so much work to help teachers understand the importance of HLA. It took me two to three years to open a new class and took forever for me to open the first HLA class in the second year. Often, other courses are deemed more important. . . . Thanks to the seal of biliteracy in New York State, which gives accountability points to the school, there is an interest. Finally, I see the students are getting the courses they need.

We may not know if it was the structural changes in programming or the changes in beliefs that first paved the way, but as the district made changes in program design, Sofia saw opportunities open up for students. Sofia paid close attention to results even when the outcome of her decisions would not come to fruition until years later, when a cohort of students would reach the completion of a course sequence or see the results at graduation years down the road.

To build the district's vision for bilingualism required more than strategic resource allocation. At the district level, it involves thinking tangibly about state mandates for units of study, program pathways, and course sequences, as well as staffing. While these are bureaucratic functions, Sofia remained focused on the student experience at the heart of program design and scheduling.

Sofia realized that there needed to be a balance between support for ELs and their integration and inclusion within school communities. The more the ENL and bilingual courses and programs grew, the more support students had access to. They experienced increased success on state exams and the accumulation of course credits, both required for graduation in their state. Students enrolling in high school programs at an older age faced challenges in meeting graduation requirements on a traditional timeline. Offering a bilingual pathway often meant that the EL students would get the support they needed but were segregated from other students, as Sofia described it, "almost a parallel school within a school."

While students were more academically successful in the bilingual pathway, they were inevitably shut out of other curricular experiences due to schedule design, class size, seats available, or other resource limitations that dictated student schedules. Sofia had to make difficult trade-offs: she could offer ELs the quickest pathway to graduation but sacrifice the rich learning experiences through elective coursework that also supports the building of community as well as non-academic skills. Another consequence of programming students into bilingual programs was that it closed them out of access to Advanced Placement classes, especially for older students who were new to the system and had less time to complete graduation requirements.

In thinking about the design of the program, Sofia needed different solutions to the students' overall academic experience so that this disparity would not ultimately be exclusionary. She found that students enrolled in the bilingual pathway, where home language was the language of instruction, were able to shine, work, and perform at the same level as their peers. However, the bilingual courses made up only a part of their school day. Sofia found that the school could integrate the students more effectively into the school community through other activities such as clubs, extra-curriculars, and sports. The Latina Heritage Club served a mixed population of newcomers and former ELs and helped students develop friendships that would have otherwise been challenging to seed. She adopted a practice from another district by integrating freshman bilingual students into bilingual health classes, where students could ask health-related questions and develop stronger relationships with teachers as mentors and engage in goal setting. Within the constraint of existing resources, Sofia's district worked around the challenges that arose from the bilingual program by ensuring that other spaces in the student experience were inclusive. In this vignette, the district's priorities implemented within a par-ticular state policy context drove the decision making. Sofia's leadership involved looking for alternative solutions within that context to still reach the vision she had for bilingual educa-tion in her district. Ultimately, each leader uses the information they have in their context to create the most optimal conditions for learning.

Sofia also experienced success in her district with the devel-opment of dual language programs in elementary schools: "We were very lucky we were able to grow the dual language program the way we have. About half of the schools have dual language, half do not; that is already a great success and accomplishment for a suburban district." The challenge for her then became hiring teachers with such a spurt of growth in these programs. In using the teachers they already had in the district, they trained them and helped with enrollment in certification programs, but as a result the amount of support teachers received would decrease. Teachers who are dual certified in language and content often lose the opportunity to work with a co-teacher in dual language classrooms, which leads to a lower teacher-student ratio.

"The ranges are tremendous because you have ELs and students with English as a home language. The levels in English and Spanish are so broad."

Despite the challenges, the benefits of implementing these programs have been significant: Sofia said, "I had one [dual language] student who loved learning the language who is now learning Spanish and is now a Spanish teacher. Many go on to become bilingual teachers and parents of bilingual students who want their kids to learn Spanish in the program." Student engagement increased through dual language programs and created new opportunities for student integration and collaboration. Sofia's advice to leaders implementing a dual language program is to work with parents and families to generate support:

> To me the most powerful thing is to work with parents. That is often why dual language programs are so successful. When you mix in parents who advocate for their kids together with parents who are new to our system, teachers and administrators respond in a different way working with parents from day one. The parents know what their rights are and what they should be expecting from teachers and administrators. To me that is the only thing that gives you a guaranteed outcome. They will be there everywhere that you cannot be. If you are going to start somewhere, I would always start there.

Discussion Questions

- ◆ What are the key challenges Sofia faced in program development?
- ◆ Consider the challenges you face in developing your own school or district's EL program. What is similar to or different from this leadership vignette?
- ◆ What are your strategies for working alongside parents and family in developing programs?

Leadership Vignette: Leading a Collaborative Model for Transformation

Leading school improvement for ELs involves skilled leadership, an ambitious vision, a sense of urgency, and moral imperative. School leaders often see the work of changing outcomes for ELs solely within the purview of the English for speakers of other languages (ESOL) or literacy educators, but when they create school-wide systems and structures, the return on investment benefits all students and educators. To establish these systems and structures we have described, a leader is also managing the change and growth process required for transformation to occur and building shared understanding across the organization to tackle challenging issues. In this next vignette, we interviewed a district leader who is working collaboratively toward this transformation with his colleagues.

When Tim Blackburn, the Title III administrator for Tigard-Tualatin District, accepted his position he didn't fully under-stand what he was getting into. He serves the Oregon district with over 12,000 students in ten elementary schools, three middle schools, and two high schools. Compliance measures for Title III can be overwhelming and greatly affect everything from how staff can be hired, the budget and resource allocation, class-room size, and teacher-to-student ratios. Even after organizing national professional learning for teachers and working both as an English language teacher and state compliance officer, he didn't fully appreciate the role until he had to take it on himself and experience the day-to-day life of the job. In addition to case management of Title III, he is also responsible for providing pro-fessional learning for all teachers in the district who serve ELs and aligning resources with services provided in collaboration with the finance and human resources teams. Tim said,

> Growing into this role, I had a healthy dose of imposter syndrome. . . . I had done this work for so long in other capacities, but the level of responsibility [is great]. Even after being a Title III compliance officer for the state of Oregon, I didn't fully appreciate this role.

He described a culture that characterized most school districts across the country, where despite good intentions, funding and staffing are often driven by traditional views of English language development, a view that has evolved since the establishment of policies over the years to include elements such as collaborative team teaching, inclusion, and integration of language development into the content areas. Tim said,

> A big part of this role is a sales job to ask everyone to challenge their schema of what English language development (ELD) is and to think and partner creatively in forming a new vision for what ELD can look like.

Tim described some of the challenges mainstream educators who are new to inclusion face in acclimating to this model and in learning new approaches to targeting what may be small groups of students in their classrooms. Another key challenge that the district faces is that, through Title III compliance, only one EL specialist per approximately 55 students is allocated. This is obviously not enough to enable collaborative team teaching in a way that truly supports the needs of ELs in integrated classrooms. In addition, reviewing and revising the master schedule with administrators at each school to enable this kind of support for ELs can be time consuming and frustrating and a problem that school teams can chip away at a little at a time. Tim shares that these common problems are part of a larger policy picture that requires educators like he and his colleagues to "present a vision for challenging the way that we have operated before." He spoke about his own vision for students in schools: "Ultimately, we want our children to have a more integrated learning experience. We don't want them to learn apart from their peers."

Despite these obstacles, Tim and his colleagues have tripled the number of co-teaching partnerships in classrooms across the district and have created a framework to document and share what it looks and sounds like to do productive collaborative team teaching that can drive professional learning for schools. Another example of success is the dual language program offered at two elementary schools, two middle schools, and one high school with plans to start a program at an additional high school. The district has helped fully staff the two-way immersion programs following a language allocation plan that was developed by the teachers and community as a guiding document to ensure that their students have a positive learning experience. In addition, the district developed an 8th grade certificate for biliteracy with a proficiency-based learning task focused on celebrating and elevating a multilingual identity. Schools conduct a small ceremony for the students as they go into 9th grade; they represent the first cohort of immersion students at this point. Tim said about this work, "Equity remains an issue with our children because we have an opportunity gap. By offering the best dual language experience programs we can, we are leveraging the assets of our students and fostering their multilingual identity by helping them learn in two languages."

Regarding how Tim handles the role, he said that he relies on his strengths as a "collaborator, listener, and convener" to celebrate others and collectively approach problem solving. A big piece of that work is defining a common vision collaboratively toward inclusive classrooms and to lower barriers or obstacles to trying out new practices and creating the right context for innovating and establishing integrative practices. He addresses this in a way that may provide insights for colleagues in a similar position.

> It is liberating to know I don't need to know all of the answers. Although I obviously need to have accountability for my role, when it comes to developing student-centered teaching and learning, that is about me creating space for my colleagues to come together and support that. [In our work in schools,] we are solving for intertwined systems and program complexities. I have come to learn it's in the collective that we accomplish the everyday wins.

For Tim and his colleagues, overcoming policy hurdles; revising the way they do assessment and instruction to be more equitable to language learners; and creating more collaborative, inclusive spaces are all part of a process. This includes not only envisioning what is possible for ELs but also finding concrete strategies in their own school contexts to enact that vision. This involves staff in teaching and learning but also those in human resources, finance, operations, and student services. In this way, building a cross-functional team that will work toward transformative change is the way that ELs will be more fully integrated and served in schools. In the next sections, we outline a few leadership behaviors that can support this transformation.

Discussion Questions

◆ What are the key challenges Tim is facing with regard to policy obstacles in his district?

◆ Consider the challenges you face in working around current local or state policies that affect your programming and staffing. What is similar or different to this leadership vignette?

◆ What are ways you already cultivate collaboration to help transform systems at your school or district? What are additional ways you might do so?

Leading Adult Development for Multilingual Learner Success

Key Action 1: Confront Institutional Bias and Deficit-Based Mindsets about ELs

One key role of the administrator is to address bias among practitioners (Benson & Fiarman, 2020; The Leadership Academy, 2020). The reality is that educators and counseling staff have room to grow in cultural competency and leadership is needed to develop culturally responsive practices and ways of thinking. In many schools, the assets and strengths that ELs bring to school communities remain unrecognized or devalued, and the minoritization of multilingual learners based on race, primary language, country of origin, religion, or other identity markers continues to perpetuate an English-only, white and middle-class dominant culture that works against the needs of culturally and linguistically diverse communities. Other deficit-based mindsets about serving ELs abound: the role of serving ELs continues to be seen as the job of the ESOL specialist rather than all teachers; the use of home language continues to be seen as a crutch rather than an essential tool for learning; ELs are continually provided with basic skill instruction as opposed to rigorous academic content; and language development continues to be seen as a barrier or problem to be solved as opposed to an asset and learning opportunity.

These biases and mindsets lead to limitations in how ELs are served. As mentioned in Chapter 3, the role division between pedagogues and counseling staff can result in teachers passing off a student's social-emotional challenges to the guidance counselor or the counseling staff misunderstanding what is required in the classroom. In these situations, it is the role of leadership to develop shared understanding among practitioners to work collectively toward a vision in which the support for ELs is broad, widespread, asset based, and consistent from every adult that works in the building. Some personnel will inevitably have more training to respond in crisis situations, but leaders can work to ensure that the responsibility and ownership of student support is collective and collaborative.

Key Action 2: Model Reflection, Personal Growth, and Cultural Competence

Another key role of the leader is to model, practice, and engage in deeper learning as a lifelong learner and educator, as they ask their school staff and personnel to do the same. Many leaders admit that they lack the experience or the expertise to lead their own communities in serving multilingual learners. Their first instinct may be to hire and expect the responsibility to fall on the shoulders of practitioners who hold implicit knowledge required to respond to the complex needs of ELs – teachers who share a student's home language or ESOL educators. Yet when leaders develop experience and invest time in building relationships with students and families, they start to see that the work of transformation is systemic. The changes involve leaders themselves systematically looking at data, reflecting on existing teaching practices, looking at evidence of student learning, and observing the implementation of professional learning. In other words, when school leaders position themselves to learn, they begin to recognize potential avenues for change within the school organization.

Key Action 3: Prioritize Adult Development and Professional Learning

As leaders develop goals and strategies to meet the needs of multilingual learners, they begin to think school-wide about how transformation can begin, and their focus should first and foremost be on adult development and professional learning to lay the groundwork for change. Leaders may have an instinct to purchase a new curriculum, to change student schedules, or to make changes in staffing or hiring, all of which are likely necessary. Yet for culturally and linguistically responsive practices to take hold, the leader will need to first identify what new learning needs to happen to strengthen the organization's capacity to serve multilingual learners. Notably, a leader is not focusing on a new metric, implementing a new practice, or rolling out a new trend in the educational landscape but instead asking questions about organizational learning and adult development (for details, see Table 5.2):

◆ *Theory of adult development* – For change to happen, school leaders need to consider their beliefs about how adults (not students) learn and grow and their role in supporting adult development. This basis for organizational learning is not always top of mind for leaders who work under intense pressure and have little time or space to reflect on their own andragogical beliefs. However, without this awareness of how the beliefs of a leader drive the culture of learning in a school, it is hard for new practices to take hold.

◆ *Professional learning experiences* – Through the design of experiential, job-embedded, teacher-centered, and teacher-led professional learning activities, leaders establish a culture of learning within the school organization that centers the needs of ELs. These activities are most effective when embedded in the ongoing work of instructional teams.

◆ *Coaching program* – It is also challenging to support changes in teacher practice without structures for coaching (Aguilar, 2019). Schools with an established coaching program are agile in their ability to incorporate culturally and linguistically responsive practices because they can use the existing spaces already carved out for observation, reflection, and rehearsal of new practices. Coaching may take place within the supervision of teachers but can also be implemented through peer coaching, teacher mentoring programs, or dedicated instructional coaching staff employed either internally or externally. Coaching is a critical component and extension of professional learning.

Key Action 4: Optimize School Operations and Human Resources for Equity

Last, a key role of school leaders is to manage logistics, operations, and administrative functions in order to tackle the deeper work of equity. Every administrator knows that technical and bureaucratic challenges are time consuming and get in the way of addressing the cultural and organizational adaptive challenges that are less urgent but extremely important. The operational aspects of each system element in and of itself can become a

Table 5.2 A gap analysis tool: Leading adult development for multilingual learner success

	Current state	**Desired state**
Theory of adult development	What is the school's theory of adult development?	What opportunities does the current approach to adult development offer to support changes in instructional practices and student support for multilingual learners?
Coaching program	What coaching framework exists to support teachers? Is the framework inclusive of a focus on equity, literacy, and multilingual learners?	What shifts can be made within the existing coaching structure to elevate the needs of ELs and attend to culturally and linguistically responsive practices? How will the school's coaching program support teachers to balance or resolve the tensions that may be inherent between their own adult development goals with the urgent needs of ELs?
Professional learning experiences	How are current professional learning opportunities designed? Is there potential within these opportunities to elevate the needs of ELs?	What shifts in professional learning topics and experiences might be needed to support school staff to engage in deeper learning of culturally and linguistically responsive practices?

barrier to organizational transformation. When administrative teams and functions do not operate efficiently, the work of developing mindsets and beliefs rarely becomes the focus of the leader's attention. Are existing systems for information sharing, communication, and timelines for key actions and tasks sufficient and adequate to support the school's objectives? What new systems might be needed in order for the school's priorities for ELs to be successful? Table 5.3 shows a few areas particularly related to multilingual learner success that school administrators can delegate to key staff, coordinate resources and communication, and evaluate the implementation.

The brief self-assessment in Table 5.4 includes key areas of leadership practice needed for multilingual learner success. Use the tool to reflect on your own leadership expertise. Then go to the Appendix D for a detailed action planning template for each systems criteria described in this book, as well as a coaching protocol that you can use to facilitate your reflection.

Table 5.3 Operational considerations for multilingual learner success

Area	Personnel	Role of Leader
Align intake, enrollment, and data systems to the workflow of administrative teams and school priorities.	Family engagement staff, parent coordinators, school records staff ESOL pedagogue, and operations supervisors	Monitor and adjust team practices to facilitate communication of real time updates relevant to intake, enrollment, and EL identification. Monitor key administrative actions and ensure information systems are updated.
Monitor student enrollment patterns and data and adjust hiring and staffing based on enrollment trends.	Hiring committee School and district leadership	Review and monitor programming and scheduling data to determine if current staffing is sufficient to provide services. Organizing hiring committees to ensure equity in hiring practices, methods of outreach, and diversify staffing to serve the student population. Liaise with district leader during hiring process and communicate job description and requirements for talent acquisition.

(Continued)

Table 5.3 (Continued)

Area	Personnel	Role of Leader
Plan for the use of Title III funding and allocate resources for English language services and professional development.	Title III coordinator, business managers, ESOL pedagogues	Use data to determine the level of instructional time needed to provide adequate services. Allocate instructional minutes to optimize English language services based on student needs.
Design master schedule with EL services in mind and align schedule to school's vision and mission for multilingual learners.	School administrators and leadership team; programming staff	Review master schedule to determine if programming supports the optimal course pathways for multilingual learners, provision of English language services, and requisite time needed for teacher collaboration.
Procure curriculum, instructional materials, assessments, and technology that are effective in supporting multilingual learners.	School administrators and leadership team	Use clear criteria and inclusive decision-making processes to determine the most high-quality materials and assessments to be purchased to serve multilingual learners. Weigh in on curriculum adoption in district or state processes to advocate for high-quality instructional materials for multilingual learners.
Secure grants or apply to grant-funded programs to support implementation of priority programs or initiatives to serve multilingual learners.	School administrators and leadership team	Use data to evaluate and determine specific areas of need. Use data to provide rationale and proposals to secure additional funding.

Table 5.4 Leadership self-assessment

For each area, choose which level best describes your current leadership practice:
Vision and purpose: Communicate a common vision and purpose for serving the ELs in your school community; clearly articulate organizational strategies for actualizing that vision.   1 Emerging   2 Developing   3 Competent   4 Advanced   5 Expert
Team learning: Develop integrated and sustainable team learning in instructional teams to drive improvement and incorporate the use of culturally and linguistically responsive practices.   1 Emerging   2 Developing   3 Competent   4 Advanced   5 Expert
School-wide integrative practices for SEL and academic instruction: Develop integrated strategies to simultaneously improve instruction and SEL based on consistent progress monitoring of students.   1 Emerging   2 Developing   3 Competent   4 Advanced   5 Expert

Culturally and linguistically responsive data practices: Implement a multilingual learner data framework to learn about students and use the data to expose inequity and improve the system. 1 Emerging   2 Developing   3 Competent   4 Advanced   5 Expert
Leadership practice and organizational strategy: Allocate resources and create connections between system elements in service of school goals for ELs; develop and monitor organizational strategies used to actualize the school's vision for multilingual learner success; design structures that support adult development. 1 Emerging   2 Developing   3 Competent   4 Advanced   5 Expert
Operations and human resources: Streamline and improve operational systems, structures, and procedures in order to efficiently and effectively provide resources and establish conditions needed to support teachers and students. 1 Emerging   2 Developing   3 Competent   4 Advanced   5 Expert

Conclusion

The system elements described in this book and the leadership practices that support them are meant to highlight effective practices we have seen through research and through our extensive experience in school support. The vignettes, scenarios, and action planning tools in this book offer glimpses into school organizations that bring together different system elements put in place by design to create equity-focused and effective programs for multilingual learner success. In Chapter 2, we described how team learning is the result of extensive leadership, training, and the development of routines and practices over time. In Chapter 3, we outlined the intensive and collaborative ways in which counseling and pedagogical staff can and need to come together to ensure that their systems and structures are responsive to the social-emotional needs of multilingual learners. In Chapter 4, we showcased schools that have incorporated a strategic set of data practices, ones that gather information not typically valued by the broader school system, with the goal of bringing to the surface the cultural and linguistic assets that multilingual learners bring to their academic careers in schools. In this last chapter, we highlighted the indefatigable work of leaders who manage and supervise the systems and structures that lead to multilingual learner success, often in difficult political environments with little support from the broader school system.

Rarely is it possible for one particular school to carry out all of the system elements we have described. The limitations that come from scarce resources do not allow for it. Leaders of school organizations operate in varied contexts and environments. They are selective and strategic about which elements are crucial for their unique context and make decisions aligned to their vision to optimize their organizational structures and existing resources. Schools do not need to have all system elements present and in place to still be able to go a long way in supporting multilingual learners in school.

References

Aguilar, E. (2019). *Why your coaching program is failing*. Education Week. www.edweek.org/education/opinion-why-your-coaching-program-is-failing/2019/08

Auslander, L. (2018). Building culturally and linguistically responsive classrooms: A case study in teacher and counselor collaboration. *Journal of Ethnographic & Qualitative Research, 12*, 207–218.

Benson, T. A., & Fiarman, S. E. (2020). *Unconscious bias in schools: A developmental approach to exploring race and racism*. Harvard Education Press.

Heifetz, R. A., Heifetz, R., Grashow, A., & Linsky, M. (2009). *The practice of adaptive leadership: Tools and tactics for changing your organization and the world*. Harvard Business Press.

The Leadership Academy. (2020). *Culturally responsive leadership: A framework for school & school system leaders*. www.leadershipacademy.org/resources/culturally-responsive-leadership-a-framework-for-school-school-system-leaders/

Appendix A
Chapter 2

In Chapter 2, we provide an example of how to organize high-performing teacher teams to include a focus on the needs of multilingual learners. Facilitators can consider the following team activities to build team collaboration and expertise in language and content integrated instruction. These experiential activities support teachers to apprentice into new pedagogical practices.

Ch. 2A Tuning Protocol for Language and Content Integration

Using a modified version of the National School Reform Faculty's Tuning Protocol, an instructional team can offer feedback to a presenting teacher on a lesson, unit, or assessment (https://schoolreforminitiative.org/doc/tuning.pdf). The presenting teacher shares an instructional objective that integrates language skills with grade-level content. When the team uses the protocol, they focus specifically on providing warm and cool feedback on the lesson, unit, or assessment with the goal of improving the way in which language skills are taught alongside academic content and how the language instruction would be embedded within the content development and disciplinary practices.

Tuning Protocol (Adapted and Modified for Multilingual Learners Based on the National School Reform Faculty Tuning Protocol, 2015)

1. Determining roles, norms, and purpose
2. Presentation
   - The presenter has the opportunity to share both the context for the work and any supporting details or documents as needed, while participants are silent.
   - Presenter should name the focus for feedback (a question or a component of the lesson) and the lesson's content and language objective.

3. Examining the work
   ◆ Group looks closely at the work, making notes on where it seems to be "in tune" or aligned with the stated goals and, guided by the presenter's focusing question and goals, where there might be a potential disconnect.
4. Clarifying questions
   ◆ The group has an opportunity to ask clarifying questions in order to better understand the work.
   ◆ The group establishes the goal and existing limitations that may impact implementation.
   ◆ Clarify questions prompt answers with quick responses (e.g., yes or no).
5. Pausing to silently reflect on warm and cool feedback
   ◆ The group individually prepares feedback. The presenter is silent.
   ◆ Identify the language demands in the lesson and where students will need support.
   ◆ Determine what language skills should be assessed.
   ◆ Provide feedback on a lesson component that develops reading, writing, or discourse skills.
   ◆ Identify when and where explicit direct instruction is needed for specific language functions and forms.
6. Tuning the lesson: warm and cool feedback
   ◆ Group shares feedback while the presenter is silent and takes notes. The feedback generally begins with a few minutes of warm feedback, moves on to a few minutes of cool feedback (sometimes phrased in the form of reflective questions), and then moves back and forth between warm and cool feedback.
7. Presenter response
   ◆ Presenter responds to the feedback and names what they will take away from the discussion.

Reference

National School Reform Faculty. (2015). *Turning protocol*. www.nsrfharmony.org/wp-content/uploads/2017/10/Tuning-N_0.pdf

Ch. 2B Student Work Analysis for Multilingual Learners

When an instructional team is new to analyzing student work through the lens of language, a facilitator may need to first provide opportunities for teachers to practice looking at language and writing practices in student work. Content teachers often focus on content accuracy. English language arts or English for speakers of other languages teachers are accustomed to looking for mastery of standards such as the use of evidence rather than looking at the particular language practices and skills – including the use of languages other than English – in academic writing. A facilitator can support an instructional team to expand their capacity to analyze student work through the lens of language development by doing practice rounds of student work analysis using protocols that direct the practitioners' attention to the language practices and strengths of the student. The instructional team surfaces what they see the student do with language, how they communicate their ideas, and what language skills the student needs to learn next. We suggest using the National School Reform Faculty's ATLAS Learning from Student Work protocol (https://schoolreforminitiative. org/doc/atlas_lfsw.pdf) with modifications to focus on the English language development framework used within the school's state context, or focus on features of language (vocabulary, syntax, sentence complexity, text structure, organization, and so on).

Student Work Protocol (Adapted and Modified for Multilingual Learners Based on the NSRF ATLAS Protocol)

1. Describe the student work.
   a. The group gathers as much information and low-inference observations about what they see in the student writing, avoiding judgements or interpretations.
   b. Describe the use of language skills, rhetorical devices, and specific ways in which the student is expressing and communicating ideas.
   c. Focus in on a specific aspect of language use (e.g., vocabulary, syntax, sentence complexity, text structure, organization) or a particular linguistic feature.
2. Interpret the student work.
   a. The group tries to find different interpretations and make sense of the student's use of language and how

they are expressing what they know. From the evidence gathered,

    i.   What is the student trying to do in this task?

    ii. What is the student doing well with language use? In this particular aspect of language use?

    iii. What is the student thinking and trying to do?

    iv. Where is the student getting stuck with language?

3. Implications for classroom practice – Based on the group's observations and interpretations, discuss the implications this work has for teaching and assessment of English learners (ELs).

    a. What specific aspects of language does the student need to learn next?

    b. What steps could the teacher take next with this student?

    c. What teaching strategies might be most effective to advance language and literacy development?

    d. What shifts in our classroom practice might be needed to be more culturally and linguistically responsive?

4. Reflect on the student work analysis.

    a. The presenter shares back what they are thinking now, what they learned about ELs or about current practices used to serve ELs or insights about looking at student work with a focus on language development.

5. Debrief the process.

    a. What do we gain by focusing on language development during the process of student work analysis?

    b. What went well? What could be improved?

    c. Facilitator can name some of the insights and observations generated through the use of the protocol that sharpens the team's diagnostic skills.

Ch. 2C Team Self-Assessment for Multilingual Learner Success

When schools have a regular practice of reflecting on their own culture, their organizational resilience and internal interconnectedness are greatly enhanced, leading to expanded capacity to address complex, adaptive challenges, such as serving culturally and linguistically diverse students. In our experience supporting instructional teams, we find that the use of team self-assessment tools to be extremely useful in surfacing important dynamics, strengths, and challenges that constitute the "work behind the work" – the underlying conditions, processes, and practices that make up how a team functions to overcome its greatest challenges and accomplish its most ambitious goals. There are many teaming self-assessment tools that exist, and a facilitator should ultimately choose one that is most suited to their community of practice.

In this assessment tool, we name key teaming indicators that we believe lead to strong instructional teams in Tables A.1 to A.7 and expand their capacity specifically in the area of language instruction and serving multilingual learners. Consider the key actions named in Chapter 2 and use the checklists below to reflect on the development of the instructional teams in your context.

Beyond the indicators of team effectiveness found in many other team assessment tools, we believe the indicators in Table A.1 to be critical for teams that serve culturally and linguistically diverse students. Table A.2 focuses on team collaboration. Table A.3 focuses on intentional team leadership. Table A.4 is a checklist for team facilitators. Table A.5 is a checklist for teams that make explicit language instruction the focus of their planning. Table A.6 is a checklist for how instructional teams learn from students and use student data. Table A.7 is a checklist for how instructional teams coordinate progress monitoring.

Table A.1 Self-assessment checklist – Focus on culturally and linguistically diverse students

Cultural and Linguistic Responsiveness	
The team . . .	**Yes/No**
actively addresses bias and deficit-thinking regarding culturally and linguistically diverse students.	
intentionally points out and celebrates students' strengths and assets when looking at student work or discussing social-emotional support.	
analyzes artifacts of student learning that reflect access to age-appropriate, rigorous, grade-level academic content (as opposed to remedial or decontextualized tasks).	
welcomes learning from student work that is written in different languages; demonstrate an appreciation for diversity in linguistic practices in English and in other languages.	
holds high expectations and aspirations for what multilingual learners can and should accomplish.	

Table A.2 Self-assessment – Collaboration

Build the Foundation of Collaboration	
The team . . .	**Yes/No**
protects time in meetings for human connection, affection, and joy.	
establishes routines for meetings aligned to the team's purpose and goals.	
plans an agenda for each meeting aligned to the needs of the team.	
collectively develops processes for shared decision making to ensure a balance of convergent and divergent thinking.	
maintains a schedule of recurring team meetings aligned to the team's needs.	

Table A.3 Self-assessment checklist – Team leadership and supervision

Develop Intentional Leadership for Instructional Teams	
The team leader . . .	**Yes/No**
creates a master schedule that allocates time, space, and staffing for the most optimal teaming structures that align with organizational priorities (e.g., grade-level, interdisciplinary, content, or teams for specific focus areas).	
provides professional learning opportunities where team leaders, facilitators, or instructional supervisors that lead teams can develop expertise in team development and team coaching.	
provides ongoing, individualized coaching and feedback to team leaders, facilitators, or instructional supervisors to support leadership development.	
leads each instructional team to establish team-specific purposes and goals aligned to school priorities.	
names and clarifies the role of each member of the team and revise roles as needed.	
develops a set of shared teaming practices that are used school-wide.	
monitors the progress of teaming structures throughout the school year and provide interventions as needed when teams face conflict or need to recalibrate.	

Table A.4 Self-assessment checklist – Team meeting facilitation

Prioritize Team Meeting Facilitation	
The team leader ensures . . .	**Yes/No**
the agenda is well planned and focused on a specific feature of instructional design.	
the tasks and questioning are aligned with the meeting agenda.	
the facilitator closely observes what team members say, think, and do and moves the team to develop a shared understanding, including healthy disagreement.	
there is a focus on evidence of student learning and the current reality.	
findings are translated into clear actions to advance student learning.	

Table A.5 Self-assessment checklist – Planning explicit language instruction

Plan Explicit Language Instruction for ELs	
The team . . .	**Yes/No**
establishes shared agreement on linguistically responsive planning and explicit language instruction as the focus of the instructional team.	
determines specific cross-discipline language skills to teach across the curriculum.	
collectively plans and designs explicit language instruction to target language skills.	

Table A.6 Self-assessment checklist – Designing instructional interventions

Learn From Students to Design Interventions	
The team . . .	**Yes/No**
determines a focal group of students to study based on team's priorities and goals.	
determines and utilizes the most effective method to analyze student work that ensures staying low on the ladder of inference and a focus on language practices.	
makes instructional decisions aligned directly with information gleaned from student work.	
asks the students to articulate their awareness of how and when to use the language skill in order to learn about their comprehension and meta-linguistic awareness.	

Table A.7 Self-assessment checklist – Progress monitoring

Progress Monitor and Determine the Impact of Instruction	
The team . . .	**Yes/No**
determines the most important data to review on a regular basis and align data systems to elevate these key information.	
creates a system that tracks progress on target language skills over time.	
uses a protocol to help the team unpack trends, connections, and insights from the data to determine impact of their instructional decisions on student learning.	

Appendix B
Chapter 3

In Chapter 3, we describe system-wide collaborative practices that bring together the perspectives of counseling and instructional staff. Here we provide a list of resources for further reading and learning in trauma-informed educational practices.

Ch. 3A Resources on Trauma-Informed Education

Crosby, S. D. (2015). An ecological perspective on emerging trauma-informed teaching practices. *Children & Schools*, *37*(4), 223–230. https://doi-org.proxy.library.nyu.edu/10.1093/cs/cdv027

Evans, J., Kennedy, D., Skuse, T., & Matthew, J. (2020). Trauma-informed practice and desistance theories: Competing or complementary approaches to working with children in conflict with the law? *Salus Journal*, *8*(2), 55–76.

Goddard, A. (2021). Adverse childhood experiences and trauma-informed care. *Journal of Pediatric Health Care*, *35*(2), 145–155. https://doi-org.proxy.library.nyu.edu/10.1016/j.pedhc.2020.09.001

Hickey, G., Smith, S., O'Sullivan, L., McGill, L., Kenny, M., MacIntyre, D., & Gordon, M. (2020). Adverse childhood experiences and trauma informed practices in second chance education settings in the Republic of Ireland: An inquiry-based study. *Children and Youth Services Review*, *118*. https://doi-org.proxy.library.nyu.edu/10.1016/j.childyouth.2020.105338

Lukens, L., & Homiak, C. (2018, March). Incorporating trauma-sensitive practices in K – 12 classrooms with refugees. *Paper presented at the annual meeting of TESOL*, Chicago, IL.

Massachusetts Advocates for Children. (2020). *Priority for trauma-sensitive remote learning: Keeping connections strong*. https://traumasensitiveschools.org/wp-content/uploads/2020/04/Trauma-Sensitive-Remote-Learning.pdf

The National Child Traumatic Stress Network. (2003). *What is child traumatic stress?* www.samhsa.gov/sites/default/files/programs_campaigns/childrens_mental_health/what-is-child-traumatic-stress.pdf

Stokes, H., & Brunzell, T. (2020). Leading Trauma-Informed Practice in Schools. *Leading & Managing*, *26*(1), 70–77.

Substance Abuse and Mental Health Services Administration. (2014). *Trauma-informed care in behavioral health services*. Treatment Improvement Protocol (TIP) Series 57. HHS Publication No. (SMA) 13–4801. Rockville, MD: Substance Abuse and Mental Health Services Administration. www.ncbi.nlm.nih.gov/books/NBK207201/pdf/Bookshelf_NBK207201.pdf

West, S., Day, A., Somers, C., & Baroni, B. (2014). Student perspectives on how trauma experiences manifest in the classroom: Engaging court-involved youth in the development of a trauma-informed teaching curriculum. *Children and Youth Services Review*, *38*(C), 58–65.

Appendix C
Chapter 4

In Chapter 4, we showcase how schools can coordinate the use of literacy, instructional, and social-emotional data sources to develop comprehensive language, literacy, and social-emotional learning support for culturally and linguistically diverse students. See Table A.8 for a sample protocol for a reading observation and Table A.9 for key factors to consider when administering reading assessments to English learners (ELs).

Ch. 4A Reading Observation Protocol

Table A.8 Step-by-step protocol for individual student reading observation

Step	Description and Details
1. Warm-up and connection.	• Ask a question to connect with the student and learn more about their interests or life updates. • Explain the purpose of the conference; reassure the student that the conference is not evaluative, and the purpose is to learn about the student's strengths and progress.
2. Student chooses a text.	• When possible, provide choices for students to select the text they read for the conference.
3. Preview the text.	• Introduce the title and author and preview text features with the student.
4. Model (if needed).	• Model the read aloud with a sentence or two; or • Model tracking the text with finger for students who are new to reading in print; or • Model the sentence pattern, if relevant to the text being used.
5. Student reads the text silently.	• Observe any reading behaviors.
6. Student reads the text aloud.	• Take notes with a running record or skill inventory. • Time the read aloud, if using rate for an oral fluency score.
7. Check oral English and comprehension.	• Use questioning to check for comprehension and prompt students to provide verbal responses.
8. Check foundational skills.	• If relevant, check for specific word recognition skills (e.g., sight words: Check for students' ability to read and translate power words for this the appropriate level).
9. Offer glows and grows.	• Name the student's strengths and assets demonstrated during the conference. • Provide the student with specific feedback based on skill inventory. Suggest active readings strategies. • Follow up on any feedback given to the student in previous conferences.

Ch. 4B Reading Assessments

Table A.9 Key considerations for using English reading assessments with ELs

Features of Reading Assessments	Considerations for ELs
Comprehension assessment	Assessments that measure text and language comprehension provide insight into whether ELs are developing the language skills needed to independently access and make meaning of a complex text in English. Allow students to provide responses in home language so that they can demonstrate their true comprehension and not be limited by having to provide a response only in English.
Oral fluency assessment	ELs benefit from developing automatic word recognition in English so that they can focus their attention on meaning. Since ELs do not initially have the same repertoire in their oral language in English as their English-only peers, assessing fluency helps teachers determine which students may need fluency instruction that has benefits for oral language development as well as being crucial for reading comprehension.
Phonemic awareness assessment	A tool that provides diagnostic information into phonological skills and word recognition in English helps teachers to determine which reading skills to teach explicitly. A phonics inventory can help rule out foundational skills as a barrier to academic literacy development, especially for long-term ELs or students with learning differences. Phonics inventories should *not* be used in isolation of comprehension assessments. This ensures that teachers confirm the reading level of a student by looking both at the student's code-based as well as meaning-based competencies in reading.
Student responses	We privilege verbal responses over written for ELs because they allow the student to answer in home language. Verbal responses allow students to express much more than they might be able to write in English. It also helps a teacher gain insight into a student's approach to problem solving with reading.
Text selection	Given the challenge of reading in a new language, assessments that utilize culturally relevant, and high-interest texts support students to fully engage in an assessment that is cognitively and linguistically demanding.
Language development versus miscues	When using any English reading assessment, it is crucial to distinguish reading errors based on a student's phonemic awareness from miscues that may in fact be natural errors related to language development. Consistent miscues may mean the student needs instruction in the skill. However, miscues related to accent, influence from their primary language, or the interaction between oral language and decoding text should be considered to accurately assess a student's strengths and needs.

Ch. 4C Writing Rubric for SLIFE and Newcomers

Writing Rubric for SIFE & Newcomer ELLs- Bridges to Academic Success

Purpose: The Bridges Writing Rubric for SIFE & Newcomer ELLs designed to assess written language development and content in English Language Arts (ELA). While designed for use in ELA, the Bridges Writing Rubric may also be applied to Social Studies writing as appropriate. If the rubric is used in Social Studies or any other content area, educators should discuss how to interpret content-area expectations before applying the rubric to student writing.

The rubric assesses content knowledge as well as English language proficiency development for students learning English. The rubric includes descriptors for six levels of development.

Key features of the Bridges Writing Rubric for SIFE & Newcomer ELLs:

- Designed for use with **SIFE** (Students with Interrupted/Limited Schooling or Newcomer students who are learning English and still need supports with foundational and early comprehension skills.
- Uses an **Assets-based** approach that focuses on what students can do.
- Divided into separate categories for **content and language** in order to provide educators with information about student development in each area.

Intended Use: The Expanded Bridges Writing Rubric is designed for use in Sheltered ENL/ELA classes or for SIFE learners who are transitioning to content area classes. This rubric is designed for regular, summative, on-demand writing and to be used as a progress monitoring tool. Appropriate uses include pre- and post-unit assessments and essay writing.

The rubric may also be used or adapted for formative, classroom-based purposes such as curriculum-embedded assessments. In these cases, it is intended to support instructors identifying students' content and language needs and strengths as they transition to mainstream content-area courses.

Instructions: To score a student response:

1. Read through the entire response to develop a sense of the overall message, language use, and style.
2. Assign scores first for Content and then for Language. Within each scoring category (Ideas, Organization, Style & Voice, Word Choice, & Sentence Fluency):
   a. Select a score level that seems to best match the response.
   b. Review the descriptor and confirm that this is a good fit for the response.
   c. If not, review other score levels to determine which score level is the best overall fit for the response.

Figure 4.1 Writing rubric for SLIFE and newcomers

Part 1: Content

This section of the rubric focuses on content knowledge in English Language Arts. **When assigning scores for Ideas, Organization, and Style and Voice, assess writing in English, another language, or multilingual responses.**

Ideas: Does the writer clearly and appropriately communicate ideas relative to the prompt?

	1 Attempted	2 Emerging	3 Developing	4 Consistent	5 Strong	6 Bridging
Clarity & Development of Ideas	Attempted expression of ideas but responses may be minimal or difficult to interpret	Expression of simple ideas with emerging clarity but intended meaning is not fully expressed and/or may be confusing to readers; Responses may be list-like or have minimal topic development	Expression of simple ideas is generally clear but concepts may not be fully developed or elaborated; Some use of support and elaboration of ideas may be present, but the reader may have to fill in gaps in meaning	Consistent expression of simple ideas with some detail and specificity; Topic development and support for ideas is often general rather than specific	Strong expression of simple ideas with detail and specificity; Some complexity is also present, but meaning may occasionally be obscured as more complex ideas are developed	Sophisticated expression of complex ideas; Meaning is generally clear even in the expression of complex ideas

(Continued)

Organization: Is the organization of the piece clear? Does the writer connect ideas logically using a variety of transitions?

	1 Attempted	2 Emerging	3 Developing	4 Consistent	5 Strong	6 Bridging
Structure & Transitions	Attempted organization but is minimal; Or organization may not be present	Emerging organization; Beginning may be implied or unclear; May lack an ending; Some transitions may be present in writing	Developing organization with a beginning and ending, and some development throughout; Uses transitions but logical connections between ideas may be missing	Consistent organization with a clear beginning and end; may be routine or formulaic; May use repetitive transitions but generally connects ideas logically	Strong organization with original and/or complex beginning and ending and development throughout; Uses a variety of transitions to connect ideas logically	Sophisticated and consistent organization throughout used to develop ideas in detail; Uses a wide variety of transitions to develop ideas and create a unified whole

Style & Voice: Is the writing tailored to the purpose and audience?

	1 Attempted	2 Emerging	3 Developing	4 Consistent	5 Strong	6 Bridging
Audience & Purpose	*Assign a score of 0 for style and voice if the response is below 4 and shows no awareness of purpose and audience.*			Writing shows limited awareness of purpose and audience	Writing shows growing awareness of purpose and audience but writing is not consistent in demonstrating this	Writing is consistently tailored to purpose and audience; Language is generally clear and engaging for the reader

Part 2: Language

This section of the rubric focuses on the development of English language proficiency. When assigning scores for Word Choice and Sentence Fluency, **you should only score the parts of the response written in English.**

Word Choice: Is there a good range of everyday and academic vocabulary and does the writer use words that convey precise meaning?

	1 Attempted	2 Emerging	3 Developing	4 Consistent	5 Strong	6 Bridging
Academic Vocabulary & Range	Uses only high frequency vocabulary	Emerging use of practiced academic words; Uses mostly high frequency and functional everyday words	Developing use of academic vocabulary and descriptive terms; Some variety in vocabulary but word choice may seem repetitive	Consistent use of relevant academic vocabulary; Uses a variety of words but may at times lack precision or clarity	Strong use of academic vocabulary to convey specific meanings; Uses a variety of words appropriately	Skillful and precise use of academic vocabulary to accomplish writing purpose; Uses a wide variety of words appropriately and to convey precision

Sentence Fluency: Does the writer construct a variety of sentences, applying forms that have been taught with accuracy?

	1 Attempted	2 Emerging	3 Developing	4 Consistent	5 Strong	6 Bridging
Sentence Structure & Variety	Uses words, phrases and short chunks of language; Frequent errors may interfere with meaning	Uses phrases and short, simple sentences; Errors may interfere with meaning	Uses mostly simple sentences and/or repetitive structures; Meaning is generally clear, but errors may interfere with meaning particularly when more complex sentences are attempted	Uses a variety of sentence types, including both simple and compound sentences; Meaning is clear although some errors may occasionally interfere with meaning	Accurately uses a variety of sentence structures; Meaning is clear, and few errors are present	Skillfully uses a wide variety of sentence structures to accomplish writing purpose; Meaning is precise and writing flows well; Few errors, even when using complex language

(Continued)

Scoring Notes:

- Assign a "0" in all categories if the response is blank, does not include any English words or is completely off-topic or irrelevant to the prompt.
- Score responses based on the evidence in the writing and not based on additional knowledge about a students' ability or proficiency. For Content (Ideas, Organization, Style & Voice), you can give credit for writing features expressed in a language other than English.
- Assign a score for each category independently of other scores. For example, a response can demonstrate strong content knowledge in Ideas, Organization, and Style & Voice and be scored at lower levels for Word Choice and Sentence Fluency if a student is in the early stages of learning English.
- Scores are assigned based on which descriptor for a category is the best overall fit for the response. A response may not perfectly match all aspects of the descriptor in order to be assigned that score.
- The rubric focuses on the development of English language proficiency and does not explicitly address writing conventions, including spelling, capitalization, and punctuation. Errors that interfere with meaning may be accounted for in scoring, but in general errors in writing conventions are not assessed when scoring Sentence Fluency because conventions are separate from writing proficiency development. The reference to "errors" in the Sentence Fluency descriptors refers to language errors. Writing conventions can be assessed separately using *Control of Conventions* criteria described in rubrics designed for the *New York State Regents Examination in English Language Arts.*

Score Calculation

CONTENT		LANGUAGE	
Ideas	_____	Vocabulary	_____
Organization	_____	Sentence Fluency	_____
Style and Voice	_____		
CONTENT TOTAL	_____	**LANGUAGE TOTAL**	_____

SCORE TOTAL (CONTENT + LANGUAGE) = _____ / 30

Figure A.1 (Continued)

Ch. 4D Read-Retell Respond Protocol for SLIFE and Newcomers

Overview of Read Retell Respond for SIFE in Mixed Settings

Students with Interrupted Formal Education (SIFE Learners) are a small minority of ELs with heterogeneous backgrounds and needs. Like all ELLs, SIFE Learners need to learn English while also learning content. However, unlike all ELLs, SIFE Learners need additional support and scaffolds to make up for their lower levels of home language literacy based on their interrupted or limited formal schooling in their home countries. While SIFE Learners bring many resources from their home cultures, they do not bring a repertoire of strategies for making meaning of text. Because they have not yet developed these in the home language, they cannot apply them to understanding text in English. For many SIFE Learners this also includes explicit instruction in literacy.

The Read Retell Respond protocol supports SIFE Learners to comprehend appropriate, stretch-level texts in English, using active reading strategies, home language, and resources. Read Retell Respond attempts to maximize student interaction with texts, with one another, and with content, as interaction is essential for learning language and making meaning.

The Read Retell Respond protocol is aligned to *The 6 Principles for Exemplary Teaching of English Learners*. These principles are based on extensive research and set an exemplary vision for the teaching of ELs, including SIFE.

The Read Retell Respond Protocol

The table below outlines steps to lead a small reading group while the majority of students work independently from you.

Student Partners	Teacher-Led Group	Notes
1. **Set purpose** by briefly connecting to Essential Question and Lesson Targets.	1. *Same*	If you have differentiated texts on the same topic, still set the purpose together as a whole class, first. Then, transition to the small reading group in step 2.
2. Students **read and annotate** the text.	2. *Teacher models and releases* annotating the text.	The type of annotation depends on the lesson target but includes translating key words and paying attention to text features.

Figure A.2 Read-retell respond protocol for SLIFE and newcomers

Bridges to Academic Success, 2019.

3. Students **listen** to text read aloud.	3. *Same*	Consider recording yourself reading the text so students can work at their own pace but still benefit from hearing the text read aloud.
4. Partners take turns **retelling in home language**.	4. *Same*	Ideally students have a home language partner. If not, encourage retelling in home language, even if to a different language partner.
5. Partners take turns **retelling in English**.	5. *Same*	Consider having students cover the text so they are not rereading but are actually retelling. They can refer to the images and glossaries for support.
6. Students complete a **thinking map** with relevant details.	6. *Teacher models and releases* adding relevant details to a thinking map.	The thinking map is determined based on the lesson target. It should be familiar to students.
7. Students **answer target question** orally and in writing.	7. *Same*	Language frames, sentences starters, and word banks can be provided to students who need them.
Extend: Students write a summary of the text.	*Extend:* Students produce a variety of sentences about the text.	There are many options for extension activities, but these are suggested because they are simple and have been successful.

Grouping Students

To determine student grouping and appropriate scaffolds, consider students' literacy levels in their home languages and their English language proficiency. In addition, leverage what you know about your specific students' strengths and needs.

Criteria	Student Partners	Teacher-Led Group
Entering English Proficiency (Beginning) *Greatly dependent on supports to advance academic language skills*		✗
Emerging English Proficiency (Low Intermediate) *Somewhat dependent on supports to advance academic language skills*	✗	✗

Transitioning English Proficiency (Intermediate) *Shows some independence in advancing some academic language skills*		×
Less proficient home language literacy level.		×
More proficient home language literacy level.	×	

*Entering, Emerging and Transitioning are all identified as having not yet met the linguistic demands necessary to demonstrate English language proficiency in a variety of academic settings.

Other strengths and needs to consider when determining groups:
- Relatedness of home language
- Background knowledge based on life experience
- Collaboration skills
- Oral English proficiency
- Entered late in unit/year
- Foundational literacy support
- Socio-emotional support

Additional Guidelines

The classroom context will determine the success of the Read Retell Respond Protocol. Below are guidelines to support teachers to foster the conditions for SIFE Learners to interact, comprehend, and write about text.
- Position the text in a thematic unit with an engaging essential question. This reinforces the purpose for reading and supports motivation.
- Model and practice the steps of the Read Retell Respond protocol, so most students have internalized that the goal of the protocol is to make meaning of text, using active reading strategies and home language. Students who have not accomplished this will be supported in teacher-led group.
- Determine flexible groups based on students' strengths and needs.
- Provide brief instruction of necessary background knowledge.
- Deliver mini lessons on high leverage forms in text and/or forms required to talk about text.
- Provide familiar thinking maps to support comprehension. Provide sentence frames and/or starters that accompany the thinking map to facilitate talking and writing about the text.
- Provides English and/or bilingual glossaries that include visuals whenever possible.
- Provide texts that are organized into manageable chunks and feature visuals that support comprehension. Differentiated texts with appropriate linguistic load are ideal. When not possible, scaffold texts to support student access.
- Integrate and reinforce the The 6 Principles for Exemplary Teaching of English Learners in your practice.

Figure A.2 (Continued)

Appendix D
Chapter 5

In Chapter 5, we share leadership stories and practices of four administrators who have made changes in their schools or districts based on a systems thinking approach and what it takes for leaders to lead reform for multilingual learner success.

Ch. 5A Action Planning Template

The Action Planning Template here includes key areas of leadership practice needed for multilingual learner success. The tool will help you reflect on your own leadership expertise as well as prompt thinking about key actions you can take in. The template includes a set of action planning questions for each of the systems criteria we described in this book.

Table A.10 is for planning a school community's overall vision and purpose. Table A.11 is used for planning and developing instructional teams. Table A.12 is for planning school-wide practices that integrate social-emotional learning (SEL) and academic instruction. Table A.13 is for planning your implementation of culturally and linguistically responsive data practices. Table A.14 is for planning leadership practice and adult development.

Table A.10 Vision and purpose

Vision and Purpose: Communicate and articulate a common vision and purpose for the English learners (ELs) in your school	
Key Questions	Your Reflection
• What are the achievement and process metrics for your ELs based on your school goals and priorities? • What are your school's greatest strengths and assets in serving ELs? • What are your school's areas of weakness in serving ELs? • What is your school community's beliefs, values, and purpose regarding serving ELs?	

Table A.11 Team learning

Systems criteria 1: Develop integrated and sustainable team learning.	
Key Questions	Your Reflection
• What does your school's professional learning curriculum look like over the course of a school year? Where are their opportunities to build in professional learning on culturally and linguistically responsive practices within instructional teams over time?	
• What are your school's instructional initiatives and how will you align professional learning objectives to serve ELs within these initiatives?	
• What are the strengths in your school's culture of learning? How can instructional teams be better leveraged to serve the needs of ELs?	
• What is the desired state of team learning in your school? How do you want teams to focus on equity and culturally responsive practices in the future?	

Table A.12 SEL and academic instruction

Systems criteria 2: Integrate SEL into school-wide structures for planning and instruction.	
Key Questions	Your Reflection
• What are your school's strengths in school-wide systems and structures for developing social-emotional learning? Do ELs benefit from these systems and structures in your school?	
• How might SEL be integrated with instruction and academic support at your school?	
• What opportunities are there to deepen collaboration between your pedagogical and counseling staff?	
• What is the desired state of collaboration between your pedagogical and counseling staff?	

Table A.13 Culturally and linguistically responsive data practices

Systems criteria 3: Establish culturally and linguistically responsive data practices to inform teaching and learning.	
Key Questions	**Your Reflection**
• What is the current approach to understanding the school's impact on learning for ELs? Does the school community have the information needed to determine if students are being served equitably?	
• How do your current data practices facilitate the use of critical information needed for culturally and linguistically responsive practices?	
• What is the desired state in terms of your school's use of culturally and linguistically responsive data? Where might you start to implement a multilingual learner data framework?	

Table A.14 Leadership practice and organizational learning

Systems criteria 4: Deepen leadership practice and organizational learning for school improvement.	
Key Questions	**Your Reflection**
• Are the leadership team's actions and strategies aligned to support your school's stated beliefs and values regarding serving multilingual learners? Where are the gaps, and what shifts in leadership practice will be needed in the future?	
• What learning experiences are needed for you and your leadership team to develop your vision and strategy for serving multilingual learners in your school?	

Ch. 5B Coaching Protocol for Self-Assessment and Reflection

Schedule a coaching session either with your leadership coach or mentor or with a trusted colleague that you feel you can be transparent and honest with to do this reflection activity with. (If you do not have a partner available to do this protocol with, use it as an individual reflection activity.) Ask your coach or partner to be a good listener, help you unpack your own thinking, and give them permission to ask you probing and powerful questions to elevate your awareness and reflection on your leadership practice. Use the Leadership Self-Assessment and the Coaching Protocol described in Figure A.3 to facilitate your coaching conversation or reflection.

1. Review each of the areas in the Leadership Self-Assessment and choose which level best describes your current leadership practice:

Vision & Purpose: Communicate a common vision and purpose for serving the English learners in your school community; clearly articulate organizational strategies for actualizing that vision 1 Emerging   2 Developing   3 Competent   4 Advanced   5 Expert
Team Learning: Develop integrated and sustainable team learning in instructional teams to drive improvement and incorporate the use of culturally and linguistically responsive practices 1 Emerging   2 Developing   3 Competent   4 Advanced   5 Expert
School wide integrative practices for social-emotional learning and academic instruction: Develop integrated strategies to simultaneously improve instruction and social-emotional learning based on consistent progress monitoring of students 1 Emerging   2 Developing   3 Competent   4 Advanced   5 Expert
Culturally and linguistically responsive data practices: Implement a multilingual learner data framework to learn about students and use the data to expose inequity and improve the system 1 Emerging   2 Developing   3 Competent   4 Advanced   5 Expert
Leadership practice and organizational strategy: Allocate resources and create connections between system elements in service of school goals for ELs; develop and monitor organizational strategies used to actualize the school's vision for multilingual learner success; design structures that support adult development 1 Emerging   2 Developing   3 Competent   4 Advanced   5 Expert

Figure A.3 Leadership self-assessment

> *Operations and Human Resources:* Streamline and improve operational systems, structures, and procedures in order to efficiently and effectively provide resources and establish conditions needed to support teachers and students
>
> 1 Emerging   2 Developing   3 Competent   4 Advanced   5 Expert

Figure A.3 (Continued)

2. Rate your level of satisfaction and efficacy in each of the areas:

   1=Emerging, 2=Developing, 3=Competent, 4=Advanced, 5=Expert

3. Looking at your ratings across the categories, consider:
   ◆ What's really working for your multilingual learners and how can your school do more of that?
   ◆ In which areas might your school community be ready to make a change?

4. Hone in on one area that feels particularly important to you to change in the near future. It should be an area that really matters to the multilingual learners in your school community. Reflect on these questions in relation to this area:
   ◆ What changes would make a difference for your multilingual learners?
   ◆ What are your school's improvement goals in this area?
   ◆ What would change in this area mean for your multilingual learners?
   ◆ What specific actions will be needed for these important changes to take hold?
   ◆ How will your leadership team be held accountable for following through on these actions?

5. Use the Action Planning Template for that particular area to flesh out your leadership strategy and key actions.

Ch. 5C Leadership Case Studies

In the following section, we developed two leadership case studies that we believe represent leadership struggles and roadblocks that many school-based leaders face as they undergo the process of leading change in their communities for multilingual learners. The leaders described are fictional, a composite of various leaders we have worked with as they embarked on their own leadership journeys. You can use a case study approach, the same as described for the leadership vignettes in Chapter 5.

Case Study #1: Leading Literacy Reform With Teams

Natalie is the assistant principal at a small size high school in a large urban district. About 11% of the students are designated as ELs, with the majority speaking Spanish as their first language and primarily black or Latinx. As the school enrolled an increasing number of students in need of English as a new language services, Natalie began to consider various strategies that could lead to improvement in student outcomes. As her leadership team reviewed reading assessment data each year, they were not seeing the growth in reading comprehension as they hoped to see for their ELs even as they saw growth for other students. With little expertise in serving ELs, Natalie wanted to better understand why the current provision of services was not adequate and what effective programs the school should use instead. She began collaborating with the principal, district staff and the ESOL specialists and convened a committee to look at the data and discuss possible program models.

After a series of meetings, Natalie led the group to inventory the state English proficiency data for all of their ELs and they drilled down to look specifically at results by students in different program models and by grade level. For individual students, Natalie started looking back at historical data for students she knew were really struggling in content classes. Using a set of data protocols with her team, she helped them to see a very different picture of their students' needs. The group realized in looking at their programming data that a number of ELs were programmed solely based on Lexile data from an English reading screener, which led to inappropriate placement of a number of ELs in a phonics-based intervention. Too few of their students were getting language services provided in core content classes as well. For long-term ELs, this resulted in stagnation in their academic literacy.

Over the course of two years, Natalie worked with her school leadership, counseling team, and English as a new language (ENL) teachers to create a set of criteria to guide them in programming students for the right kinds of support. They hired additional qualified English for speakers of other languages (ESOL) certified teachers. Students were no longer programmed for phonics interventions. The teachers created additional courses in which students could receive language services and elective credit, in addition to having core content courses taught by dual certified staff. The changes to the program model and schedule allowed the school to align student schedules more closely to their needs. Even with these positive changes, Natalie knew that the programming options were only one way to tackle how to serve her school's ELs. She knew the teachers in the school were very far away from feeling confident in their ability to effectively serve the students.

So, Natalie began facilitating weekly meetings not only with the ESOL teachers but also with the other literacy specialists in the building. In the fall, Natalie used a data protocol with the group to closely analyze all of the data sets utilized by their school and drilled down to a small group of ELs who struggled with academic success more broadly and in multiple classrooms. The team responded really well to these meetings, and they felt a sense of urgency to help the students. They started brainstorming ideas, and they made a list of instructional resources that the team could access and that they felt would benefit their students.

Although the initial team meetings were successful, after a few months, Natalie realized the team was stuck. A number of meetings were cancelled due to school-wide events, and for the meetings that were held, Natalie was not able to attend all of them. Natalie knew she had to figure out where to take her team next to get back the momentum they started with. She knew she wanted the team to start problem solving and identify the root of where these students' struggles were. She was hoping that the team could deepen their understanding of the students' needs by interviewing the students, doing reading conferences with the students, using student observation protocols to shadow students in different classroom settings, and monitoring key pieces of data over time such as attendance and pass rates in core courses. Moving forward, Natalie knew she had to be more vigilant in her leadership to plan the team meetings and figure out what they really could accomplish together as a group.

Discussion Questions

- ◆ Why did the team get stuck? What were the key problems or issues relevant to the development of this team?
- ◆ What does Natalie need to do as a leader to move forward with the vision she already has for the team?
- ◆ What recommendations would you give to Natalie as an assistant principal in this scenario? What key questions should she consider?

Case Study #2: Journey of a Literacy Coach

Emily was a newly hired school-based instructional coach at a school that consisted of approximately 55% ELs. With a majority of ELs, teachers at the school had a lot of expertise in scaffolding for the students, teaching language along with content, and creating culturally sustaining learning environments where students celebrated their cultures and identities in various ways throughout the school day and during school-wide events and rituals. When Emily started coaching at this school, about 23% of the students who were ultimately able to graduate from the school required remedial courses in English. The principal saw this as a major area in need of improvement. While many teachers though that it was already an achievement that the students were able to graduate from high school as ELs, the principal believed the school was not doing enough to help students adequately prepare for post-secondary literacy. Emily was tasked with helping the principal develop a long-term plan to meet this larger goal.

By the end of the first trimester, Emily had enrolled a number of teachers to work with her as an instructional coach. She had developed trusting relationships with a few teachers and collaborated with them on a weekly basis to plan lessons with literacy strategies to be used with content instruction, observed classes, and debriefed the lessons with teachers. Emily also worked with another group of teachers less frequently and with whom she knew she faced significant skepticism. These teachers enrolled to work with her as a coach but presented a lot of push-back when Emily made suggestions to address literacy skills among the students in these teachers' classes. Emily knew the school would not improve their literacy instruction if the knowledge and practices were not more widespread.

Emily created a proposal to the principal and the committee of lead teachers at her school to implement a professional learning arc for the next few months. She and one or two other teachers passionate about literacy would facilitate four interconnected workshops for the whole staff with the goal of helping teachers interpret and analyze literacy data that was collected and develop teachers' understanding of practices that would support students who were most at risk for reading struggles. After the first session, while a majority of staff felt it was a meaningful workshop, most expressed resistance to the idea of spending time to look at the data, and most did not seem interested in implementing the new strategies that Emily presented. Emily and the other teachers on the planning committee only ended up facilitating one other session for the school instead of the full curriculum they had hoped to implement. At the end of the year, the principal complained that they had invested a lot of time in assessing students with reading assessments, in creating systems to organize and visualize the data, as well as precious professional learning time with the whole staff. She lamented that she did not see the results that she hoped for and started second guessing the initial direction the school took related to literacy reform.

Emily felt frustrated because she thought that she had to fight many battles to advocate for students with reading struggles to persuade teachers to recognize the urgency and importance of responding to gaps in reading skills. She realized she had to go back to the drawing board to figure out how she would help her school move toward their ultimate goal of supporting students to become confident readers with advanced and academic literacy.

Discussion Questions

- ◆ What key cultural or political problems or issues did Emily face as a literacy leader?
- ◆ What conditions would have to be in place in order for this school to be able to shift in the direction the principal hoped for?
- ◆ What did Emily and the principal need to do together as literacy leaders in order to move their school toward the vision they hoped for?
- ◆ What recommendations would you give to Emily as an instructional coach in this scenario?
- ◆ If you were coaching Emily, what questions might you ask her?

Printed in the United States
by Baker & Taylor Publisher Services